# STRANGE & UNUSUAL
## SHIPWRECKS ON THE GREAT LAKES

### WAYNE LOUIS KADAR

D1568991

Avery Color Studios, Inc.
Gwinn, Michigan

©2007 Avery Color Studios, Inc.

ISBN-13: 978-1-892384-41-6
ISBN-10: 1-892384-41-8

Library of Congress Control Number: 2006940491

First Edition 2007
10   9   8   7   6   5   4   3

Published by
Avery Color Studios, Inc.
Gwinn, Michigan 49841

Cover photos: the *Christopher Columbus,* from the photographic collection of the Port Huron Museum; artist's concept of the *D.L. Filer;* a Great Lakes steamer from the State of Michigan Archives, Lansing, Michigan; the German submarine *UC-97,* from the collection of Leonard DeFrain. Back cover: the original Houghton swing bridge, courtesy of the Houghton County Historical Society.

No portion of this publication may be reproduced, reprinted or otherwise copied for distribution purposes without written permission of the publisher.

*I dedicate this book to the men and women of museums, historical societies, libraries, and individuals who strive to preserve the rich nautical heritage of the Great Lakes.*

*One of those individuals I specifically want to thank is Hugh Clark, for allowing me access to his personal Great Lakes Photographic Collection, and for being a mentor and a great friend.*

# TABLE OF CONTENTS

# INTRODUCTION

Any shipboard disaster, be it a collision, capsizing, fire or any other equally horrific event is tragic. Vessels, crew, cargo, and passengers are potentially lost. Yet the cause and results of some Great Lakes maritime mishaps are interesting and educational due to conditions which surround the event.

Shipwrecks are the result of many causes. Some are mysterious in nature, some are surrounded by strange occurrences, and still others are maritime events that are weird, bizarre, foolish and sometimes dumb.

Some ships have shoved off from the dock never to be seen again. They simply sail off into oblivion. They leave no telltale debris trail, no clue as to their demise; all that remains are questions. Some other strange

1

wrecks involve maritime events of unusual circumstances. The unusual circumstances might be freakish weather patterns, strangely re-occurring events or other unique and unusual situations.

There are also shipwreck accounts, which leave the observers scratching their head wondering, "What were they thinking?"

An example of one such maritime incident stands as a tribute to mankind's thought and/ or thoughtlessness. It seems the owner of a trailer-able recreational boat had to move the boat and trailer from one location to another. Rather than pull the boat and trailer behind his vehicle he decided to power the boat and trailer to the new location.

Today the boat, still firmly strapped to the trailer, is lying on the bottom of Lake Superior. "What was he thinking?"

All accidents involving vessels on the Great Lakes are terrible and tragic. The intent of this book is not to make light of someone's loss, but rather to educate others about how the maritime disasters have occurred.

# THE STORM OF SEPTEMBER 1930

**T**he Great Lakes are notorious for storms which can produce hurricane force winds, blinding snow, and tremendous seas. Some storms are short-lived squalls yet some stall over the Great Lakes basin and lay siege to the area for days.

One storm that assaulted the Great Lakes isn't as well known as the Great Storm of 1913 or the Armistice Day storm of 1940, but a storm that stands out in the annals of the lakes. It is the September 1930 storm that unleashed its fury on Lake Michigan.

The weather system approached from the southwest with terrible thunderstorms, severe lightning and 49 mile per hour winds. The storm raised havoc for nearly 24 hours before it passed over.

Barns collapsed, roofs were ripped off, windows were blown in, trees uprooted and toppled, power poles snapped and farmer's crops were ruined.

On Lake Michigan the storm produced towering waves, reaching 30-feet high, or taller than a three-story building!

The fruit packet, *North Shore*, departed St. Joseph, Michigan with a cargo of 10,000 pounds of grapes bound for Milwaukee, Wisconsin.

X– Our Son

## Most Severe Gale Recorded Locally Causes Much Lo...

Sweeping up from the southwest and accompanied by torrential rains and severe lightning, a 49-mile gale, the ... ever recorded here, struck this district Friday morning ... cunning untold loss on lake and land.

For nearly 24 hours the gale continued with hardly ... sewed fury before it moved northeastward, toward Canada ...

**Strikes in All Quarters.**

Orchards, farms, resort properties, city properties, lines of communication and shipping were heavily damaged. The gale, whose velocity of 49 miles was equal to 60 ... under the former weather bureau system of measure ... was companioned by a 25-degree drop in temperature, ... ing householders to start grate and furnace fires.

### HALF OF APPLE CROP IN COUNTY RUINED BY FURIOUS STORM

Appalling Damage Is Done to Fruit by Friday's Gale.

Is Worst Storm in History, as Far as It Affects Fruit, Says L. A. Hawley.

Total rainfall was 1.09 ... effectively ending the ... drought and having one ... ficial effect, that of ... the forest fire menace.

Local shipping ... home port Friday. Car... entered harbor shortly ... noon Friday. Outbound ... were held, three in L... one in Milwaukee and ... Manitowoc, none. Boat ... 7 o'clock Saturday morning ... regular schedule, ... Mercereau stated yesterday being resumed as rapidly ... sible.

Epworth Cottages ... Epworth Heights ... the full fury of the high ... Portions of roofs of 30 ... were torn off and ... yesterday were ... the damage. Trees ...

*A headline from the* Ludington Sunday Morning News.

The ship carried a crew of six including Captain E.J. Anderson, and his bride of two weeks.

The *North Shore* did not arrive in Milwaukee nor did she return to St. Joseph. It was hoped that the ship had made it to another port or had sought refuge in a deserted cove.

Hope for the *North Shore* was abandoned when large quantities of grape baskets washed up on shore.

The ship and the crew of the *North Shore* were never seen again.

Another victim of the September 1930 storm was the stone barge *Salvor*. The barge, equipped with a tall derrick shovel, drifted helplessly in the teeth of the storm after it broke loose from its tug north of Muskegon, Michigan.

As the storm shoved the drifting barge at will, seven of the crew took to the life raft. Several of them tied themselves in the raft to keep from being washed out by the waves.

Three men took their chances on the deck of the barge while two others of the crew climbed the derrick.

# TOLL OF FRIDAY'S STORM ON LAKE MICHIGAN NOW 11 DEATHS AND LOSS OF THREE VESSELS

Definitely Established Fruit Boat, North Shore, Went Down with Crew of Five Men and One Woman; Three Investigations in Salvor Wreck Indicated.

*A headline from the* Muskegon Chronicle.

*The Harbor Beach Coast Guardsmen practice using the Breeches Buoy. From the Grice House Museum, Harbor Beach, Michigan.*

The men huddled on the deck were assaulted by the waves crashing over the barge and one by one were ripped from the *Salvor*. The two men clinging to the girders of the derrick hung on as the storm raged, pushing the stone barge north until it grounded a distance from shore.

The Muskegon Coast Guard was notified that the *Salvor* had grounded and was being viciously assaulted by the storm whipped waves. The Coast Guard quickly pulled their shore apparatus to the beach near the grounded barge. When they arrived they found wreckage littering the beach and bodies of several men washed up on shore.

The Coast Guardsmen quickly set up the Lyle Gun and shot the line towards the disabled vessel. The purpose of the Lyle Gun was to shoot a projectile attached to a light line to the vessel. The crew on the ship would then pull the light line, which was attached to a heavier line, to the ship. Once the heavy line was secured to the ship and to shore, a breeches buoy would be used to carry the crew to safety. The breeches buoy is a ring buoy hung horizontally from the heavy line. Attached to the ring buoy is what is best described as a rubber pair of pants. The men on the stricken ship would climb into the breeches buoy and the Coast Guard would pull them along the heavy line to shore.

Unfortunately, all three attempts of the Coast Guard fell short of the stone barge *Salvor*. The ship was too far from shore to shoot a line to them with the wind blowing in from the southwest. Rescue of anyone left onboard would have to be made in a different manor.

Captain Preston and a crew from the Grand Haven Coast Guard Station set out into the storm at 4:00 am the following morning. The storm had not subsided and the Coast Guard crew in the open lifeboat met with difficulty in transit to the disabled stone barge. The winds had swung around to the west and the guardsmen took the full brunt of the storm on their beam for the entire two-hour trip to the *Salvor*.

When they arrived at the grounded barge, Captain Preston at the tiller skillfully navigated the lifeboat around the floating debris to get near the stricken craft. They looked for any survivors who may remain on the ship. Huge waves broke over the barge preventing the heroic men in the lifeboat from getting very close.

The Coast Guardsmen were about to give up hope when they saw movement from one of the men strapped in the derrick of the steam shovel. Knowing that there was at least one life to save, the Coast Guardsmen renewed their efforts. Unable to get close to the violently

*The sailing vessel* Our Son *caught out on Lake Michigan during the September 1930 storm. From the State of Michigan Archives, Lansing, Michigan.*

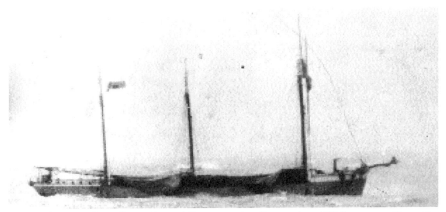

*The Schooner* Our Son *after riding out the September 1930 storm. Note the American flag flying upside down as a signal of distress. The ship later sunk to the bottom of Lake Michigan. From the State of Michigan Archives, Lansing, Michigan.*

rocking barge, Captain Preston yelled to the men in the derrick to jump into the water and they would pull them out.

The men, numbed by the cold, their 15-hour fight in the storm and sheer fright did as they were told and jumped. The water was churning all about them as they hit the water. They frantically swam towards the lifeboat and the heaving line the Coast Guard had thrown. The two men were rescued from an almost certain death.

Twenty miles off Ludington, Michigan the crew of another ship was fighting for their lives.

The ship was the 182-foot long, three-mast schooner, *Our Son*. Returning from Manitou Island with a load of pulpwood bound for the Central Paper Company of Muskegon, Michigan, the ship battled the huge waves. The schooner, not equipped with auxiliary power, was at the mercy of the winds in her sails.

The violent storm blew most of her sails to tattered shreds and the ship wallowed helplessly in the huge waves. Captain Fred Nelson, the 75-year-old master of the vessel, ordered the distress flag to be flown and hoped another ship would happen by and see their peril.

The crew could do nothing but hope and pray.

Also on Lake Michigan during the horrific storm was the steamer *William Nelson*. The *Nelson* was heading to Indiana Harbor, Indiana, when in the distance she saw the schooner drifting in the storm, their American flag flying upside down as a distress signal.

# CREW OF OUR SON TAKEN FROM HISTORIC SHIP IN THRILLING AND DARING SHOW OF SEAMANSHIP

Master of Nelson Makes Rescue at Risk of Own Boat as Waves Beat Craft

## SCHOONER SINKS

Last of Sailing Vessels on Great Lakes Goes Down in Storm Still Fighting.

*A headline from the* Muskegon Chronicle.

Captain C. A. Mohr, Master of the *Nelson*, at great risk to his own vessel, circled back to assist the schooner. When in hailing distance, sailors of the steamer yelled to the schooner to come into the wind. Lifeboats were readied on the *Nelson* but launching a lifeboat in these conditions would be suicide. The only chance for the *Nelson* to rescue the crew of the *Our Son* was to nose up to her and have the crew jump aboard.

The waves crashed on the steamer, trying to push it off course as it inched nearer the drifting ship. A tremendous wave broke on the ship, ripping away one of the lifeboats and tossing it into the lake where it was smashed by the waves. At risk to his own ship, Captain Mohr maneuvered the *Nelson* along side the schooner; the bow of the bounding steamer slowly eased up to the schooner and with the help of the steamer's crew the seven sailors of the schooner and her captain were able to jump to safety aboard the steamer. In keeping with the tradition of the Lakes, Captain Fred Nelson was the last to leave the ship.

As the *William Nelson* steamed away, the crew of the schooner watched their boat until it disappeared.

The schooner *Our Son* went to the bottom of Lake Michigan on that 26th day of September in 1930. The *Our Son*, launched in 1875, was the last of the old-time sailing vessels. When she went down it ended the era of the sailing schooner carrying cargo on the Great Lakes.

# A STRANGE ACCOUNT FROM THE STORM OF 1913

**O**ne of the most treacherous of storms ever to attack the lakes has become known as the "White Hurricane."

The date was November 9, 1913, when the storm of the century first struck the Great Lakes and left in its wake, more than forty ships damaged, destroyed or sunk and at least 235 sailors dead.

On Saturday, November 8, 1913 there was a fall storm blowing on Lake Superior, which is typical for the season, although this storm was unusual for its strength. Blowing from the west with heavy snow, eastbound ships were running with following seas, and westbound vessels took it on the nose.

On 365 mile long Lake Superior, the winds blew from the west along its length, unobstructed, building in velocity and creating huge seas. The winds on November 8, 1913 were reported at a velocity of 68 miles per hour. Most ships, except the largest and most powerful, sought the shelter of a harbor or in the lee of an island or other land mass. Those ships that continued out in the lake were tossed about like corks in the blinding storm. When it reached the eastern end of Lake Superior another weather system over the

**9**

east coast caused the storm to turn to the south, taking aim for Lake Huron.

On Lake Huron at the tip of Michigan's Thumb, the keeper of the Port Austin Reef Lighthouse recorded in the lighthouse journal for November 9th that everything was normal. Wind from the south with rain, a temperature of 40 degrees and a barometer reading of 29.18. It was

# MANY SHIPS AT MERCY OF WIND AND SEA

### Never in Marine History Have Lakes Been Lashed Into Such Fury and Anxiety Is Felt For Many Vessels Which Have Not Yet Reported

*A headline from the*
Port Huron Times Herald.

cooler than the 60 degrees of the day before and a slight drop from yesterday's barometer reading of 29.22, but that was expected in late November.

A day later his journal entry was much different.

"Sounding for snow, biggest sea running I ever see at this station."

During those fateful few days in November of 1913 there were three weather patterns developing in separate parts of the country. A low pressure system followed by cold arctic air was moving east across the length of Lake Superior. At the same time a subtropical low pressure system was moving northward through the southeastern states. The third system over the east coast prevented the other systems from moving on; the combined storms hung over the Great Lakes.

The northern storm changed directions when it reached Sault St. Marie and turned south over upper Lake Huron. The cold arctic storm stalled at that point and would linger over Lake Huron for the next three days. The moisture laden southern storm reached Lake Huron and combined with the northern weather system. The result was a storm of cataclysmic proportions, a storm which has been called the worst storm ever on the Great Lakes; a "White Hurricane".

The ships in the open water of Lake Huron were subjected to horrendous conditions. Waves of 30- and 40-feet were confronted, as well as wind gusts as high as 80 MPH. Steady winds of 75 MPH, as recorded in south Lake Huron, were common and visibility was severely limited due to the heavy blowing snow.

# A STRANGE ACCOUNT FROM THE STORM OF 1913

One can only imagine the horror the crews of the ships caught out in the storm experienced. The mighty steel ships were assaulted by the winds blowing anything not secured into the angry lake. The huge ships rose and crashed down on waves which crested the size of a four story building. Their prow would plow headlong into the wall of water, the windows of the pilothouse and the structure itself would creak and moan with the onslaught, threatening to be broken away. The wind howled and whistled through any opening in the ship.

Crewmen huddling in the cabins could hear the terrible sound of lines snapping and the screeching sound of metal being twisted and broken as lifeboats, hawser pipes, and stacks were ripped from the vessels and washed away.

Two of the big ships lost on November 11, 1913 were the *Charles S. Price* and the *Regina*.

At 269-feet, the *Regina* was one of the smallest ships to venture out on the lake that day. The nearly new vessel was making her way south with a load of steel pipe and a crew of 20.

The *Charles S. Price* was one of the kings of the lakes; only three years old and a huge 524-feet in length. The *Price* was up bound on Lake Huron with a load of coal and carried a crew of 28.

No one will ever know for sure what happened that fateful day of November 11, 1913. What is known is the crews of both vessels were lost.

*The 269-foot steamer* Regina *sank with all 20 hands during the storm of November 1913. From the collection of the Port Huron Museum.*

*The 524-foot* Charles Price. *From the State of Michigan Archives, Lansing, Michigan. From the collection of the Port Huron Museum.*

Almost as soon as the big *Price* entered Lake Huron from the shelter of the St. Clair River, she was assaulted with 50 – 75 mile per hour winds and seas approaching 35-feet in height.

The captain of the *Price* saw that conditions were not to his liking. He decided to come about and return to Port Huron and the safety of the St. Clair River.

It's not known how far north the ship traveled before coming about. Had they made the 30 miles to Lexington, the 45 miles north of Port Huron to Port Sanilac? Or had they traveled as far as Harbor Beach, some 60 miles to the north?

The *Regina*, down bound on the lake, made it as far south as Harbor Beach before the vessel, beat by the huge waves, succumbed to the storm and foundered.

What happened to the *Charles S. Price* is still a question. All that was known for sure is that she was found floating, hull-up, near the south end of Lake Huron. Possibly when she turned to come about she was trapped in the trough of the huge waves and capsized.

Tom Reid, of the Reid Wrecking and Towing Company, headquartered in Sarnia, Ontario, got a call from the Fort Gratiot Coast Guard Station along the south shore of Lake Huron. The Coast Guard had received messages that a big steamer was on the lake and in trouble. They told Tom that they couldn't go out; their boats had been smashed and wrecked by the storm. They asked if Tom could respond.

# A STRANGE ACCOUNT FROM THE STORM OF 1913

*The capsized hulk of a Great Lakes steamer was found floating in lower Lake Huron. From the State of Michigan Archives, Lansing, Michigan.*

At dawn Tom Reid was on his tug *Sarnia City*, leaving the relatively calm waters of the river heading straight into the teeth of the storm on the lake. They passed the *Huron Lightship*, usually anchored on Corsica Shoals to guide ships into the narrow channel leading to the river, but the lightship had been blown off position and was at anchor trying to stay out of the shallows.

As the *Sarnia City* proceeded north in the wicked storm, they saw the 600-foot southbound *Matthew Andrews* struggling to make the river. Tom Reid watched through the glasses as the ship drove up on the sand bar. She had grounded before reaching the safety of the river.

The *Sarnia City* continued north, battling the wind and huge seas, until they came upon the ship they were sent out to assist. They saw a steel hull of a steamer, a big one, upside down, bobbing in the violent lake, only the bow above the surface. There wasn't anyone to be found, there was nothing they could do. The wreckers would have to wait until the storm blew itself out before they could do anything.

Among the waterfront bars there was much speculation as to which ship Reid had found. With ten large steel freighters lost on Lake Huron during the three day storm, there were many possibilities.

When the weather calmed, the *Sarnia City* again went to the capsized hull. Lewis Meyers donned the hard hat diving suit and under the supervision of Tom Reid was lowered down to determine the name of the mystery vessel. He came up with the news; *Charles S. Price*.

The *Price*, only three years old, had "turned turtle" in the violent storm of November 1913, a testament to the strength and fury of the storm. Her crew of 28 had perished in the disaster. In the following days their bodies began washing up on the Canadian shore.

As the bodies were found, a mystery that would perplex Great Lakes historians and sailors alike for decades was revealed. On the shore, crew known to be aboard the *Charles S. Price* were found wearing life preservers from the *Regina*!

This led to much speculation. Had the two ships collided during the storm, and some of the *Price* crew jumped to the *Regina*?

Another theory trying to explain the life jacket question was that possibly the men of the *Price* were cast adrift after their ship had capsized. They were rescued by the *Regina* and given life preservers.

*It was a Reid Wrecking and Towing Company diver that was sent down to determine the name of the mystery ship. From the State of Michigan Archives, Lansing, Michigan.*

Still there was another possibility presented. Possibly crew from both ships had been found on the beach and locals, in the process of robbing the bodies of their belongings, were scared away from their dastardly deed and put the wrong life preserver on the wrong body.

Whatever the cause of the mystery, the answer has never been found; it has been perpetuated for over 90 years. None of the sailors lived through the catastrophe so no one really knows.

# SHIPS AND BRIDGES; HOUGHTON/HANCOCK

**A** look at a map of Lake Superior reveals the Keweenaw Peninsula as the most prominent feature of the lake. Ships traveling the southern shore of Lake Superior from the Soo Locks toward Duluth, Minnesota, or in reverse, would have to head north around the peninsula then head south, but ships can cut over 100 miles off the trip by cutting across the Keweenaw Peninsula through the Portage Ship Canal.

The canal was completed in 1874 by blasting out a 2 mile long, 100-foot wide, and 14-foot deep waterway through the rock connecting Lake Superior at the west and Portage Lake on the east side of the peninsula. The Portage River leading from Portage Lake to Lake Superior was then widened and deepened to complete the canal.

Along the canal are two major Upper Peninsula cities; on the south side is the city of Houghton, Michigan and on the north is Hancock, Michigan. In 1875 a swing bridge was built across the canal to connect the two cities. The bridge was built with two levels, the lower for railroad traffic and the upper for street traffic.

When a ship approached the bridge they blew the signal to open, 4 blasts on the steam whistle. The

X--Houghton / Hancock

**15**

*The original Houghton Swing Bridge open for a steamer to pass through. Courtesy of the Houghton County Historical Society.*

Bridge Engineer would then turn the wheel which released the latch which held the span in position. The bridge would pivot on its center piling creating an opening for the ship to pass through.

On April 15, 1905 the 30-year-old bridge met with the bow of a Great Lakes steamer. On that day, at 4:30 in the afternoon, pedestrians strolled across the bridge, railroad traffic crossed the span on the lower level while a steamship approached the bridge.

Captain Carringway of the *Northern Wave* of the Mutual Transit Company, directed his ship along the canal slowly approaching the bridge. He sounded the four blasts on his whistle informing the bridge engineer to open for his intention to pass through.

Daniel Hardiman, the bridge engineer, looked out from the bridge at the approaching vessel. He awaited the signal to activate the bridge swing mechanism. The ship continued towards the bridge when finally the whistle sounded… three blasts; the signal of the ship's intention to dock.

Mr. Hardiman continued watching the steamer. It didn't seem to be on a course towards the dock, rather it continued towards the bridge. Fearing the ship might have signaled in error, the bridge engineer began to open the bridge but the catches which hold the span in position would not quickly unlatch.

Mr. Carringway saw a pedestrian on the bridge, Ralph DeMary, and called for his help. The two men grasped the wheel, and with their combined strength tried to free the catches. The catches refused to open.

*A photograph of the original Portage Ship Canal. From the collection of Chuck Voelker, CopperCountryReflections@pasty.com.*

The steamer continued to bear down on the bridge. Pedestrians looked on in horror and began to run for points of safety. With a screech of metal against metal filling the air, the pedestrians watched the steamer ram into the swing bridge. The impact caused the bridge to topple over at its pivot point.

With the amount of pedestrians that were on the bridge that day it is a miracle that there were only two injuries. Bridge engineer Carringway and Mr. DeMary were both hurt when they were thrown against the metalwork as the *Northern Wave* slammed into the bridge.

At once the captain claimed the incident was caused by the bridge engineer; he had sounded the mandatory four blasts and the bridge had not opened. Mr. Carringway claimed that the ship had only sounded three blasts, a fact that was substantiated by many of the bridge pedestrians.

With the bridge in ruins, the Mineral Range and Copper Range railroads were the most impacted. They could not easily transport their cargos across the canal, and residents of both cities were also affected by the loss of the bridge because the Houghton County Street Railway traffic across the bridge had to be suspended.

Repairs on the swing bridge were begun at once.

The bridge was repaired by the next spring and it once again carried pedestrian, carriage and railroad traffic across the Portage Ship Canal.

*The wreckage of the Houghton Swing Bridge after the* Northern Wave *rammed the bridge. The turntable on which the swing bridge rotated is clearly seen. Courtesy of the Houghton County Historical Society.*

*A similar swing bridge, in the open position, crossing the Fox River at Green Bay, Wisconsin. The photograph was taken from the deck of the tall ship* Highlander Sea. *The author is a volunteer crew member of the ship.*

The bridge operated another 53 years without further major mishap. But, in 1959 the old swing bridge was showing wear and its age. It was deemed necessary by State maritime and highway officials that a new bridge had to be built to accommodate larger ships which were plying the Lakes and the automobile and truck traffic.

State of Michigan engineers made a study and recommended that a vertical lift bridge would be the best form of convenience across the river.

The Houghton vertical lift bridge was completed and opened in December of 1959 and the dedication celebration of the new bridge was scheduled for June 25, 1960.

The celebration was going to be a huge event. High school bands would play. Politicians would be there for photo opportunities and even a fly-over by the United States Air Force was scheduled.

The day before the dedication celebration, the 557-foot, 53 year-old Great Lakes freighter *J.F. Schoellkopf Jr.* was on the canal approaching the new lift bridge.

Following proper protocol, Captain Wilhelmy of the *J.F. Schoellkopf Jr.* sounded the whistle signaling the bridge to open. The ship proceeded on towards the bridge. The captain watched to see the bridge open but it didn't. Possibly the bridge operator was waiting for traffic to clear before the blinking red lights were turned on and the gates closed.

The captain and wheelsman watched intently for the bridge to begin the opening process. A Great Lakes freighter requires miles to stop.

*Another view of the wreckage of the bridge after the steamer* Northern Wave *collided with it. Courtesy of the Houghton County Historical Society.*

*Construction of the new vertical lift bridge across the Portage Ship Canal. Courtesy of the Houghton County Historical Society.*

Stopping and waiting for the bridge to open was not an option. The bridge had better open soon.

Additional soundings on the whistle did not result in the bridge opening. "Maybe they are having troubles," thought the captain. Captain Wilhelmy knew he had better take measures.

"Reverse full!"came the order.

The Captain knew it was necessary to stop the forward momentum of the ship. If not his ship would crash into the brand new $11 million Houghton vertical lift bridge, and on the day before its Grand Opening celebration.

Captain Wilhelmy watched out the windows of the pilothouse. The bridge was not raising, nor did it appear that there was any attempt to open the bridge. There were no bells, no flashing lights, no road traffic barricades lowered, pedestrians and automobile traffic continued across the span.

A collision between the steel bridge and the *J.F. Schoellkopf Jr.*, even with the ship at a reduced speed and in reverse would be catastrophic. In a best case scenario the roadbed of the bridge would be bent and broken and the bow of the ship would be damaged. In the worst case, the roadbed would be ripped from its two supporting towers and pushed into the waterway, the towers would be pulled from their foundations and crash into the canal on top of the roadbed. The bridge would be destroyed and the waterway blocked by the debris, leaving the canal un-navigable for months.

The loss of life could be extensive as the pedestrian and automobile traffic, not stopped by barricades, drove off the bridge into the water below.

Damage to the *J.F. Schoellkopf Jr.* had the potential to be devastating as well. The *J.F. Schoellkopf Jr.*, being a ship of its era, was constructed with the pilothouse at the bow, unlike the modern Great Lake freighters which are piloted from the stern.

A collision with the Houghton vertical lift bridge could severely damage the forward structure leaving the 53 year-old vessel too expensive to repair. The once proud *J.F. Schoellkopf Jr.* would probably finish out its usefulness on the lakes as a barge, as a floating storage container or it would be towed to the salvage yard to be scrapped.

Captain Wilhelmy watched the bridge as his ship bore down on it. The order to reverse had slowed the ship but still a collision was imminent.

"Lower the anchors!"Captain Wilhelmy shouted to a deckhand standing at the ready.

The anchors splashed into the canal and the heavy chain roared as it was payed out.

The anchors dragged along the bottom, the *J.F. Schoellkopf Jr.* continued forward towards the bridge. Suddenly the anchor chain snapped taut. The anchors held fast to the bottom and stopped the ship, averting what could have been a major maritime disaster.

The quick thinking and actions of the captain were responsible for preventing the collision. He responded by reversing the engine and

*The 557-foot* J.F. Schoellkopf Jr. *From the Hugh Clark Great Lakes Collection.*

dropping the anchors. The anchors dragged until the hooks snagged two submarine telephone cables traversing the Portage canal.

The Grand Opening celebration took place the following day. Many of those attending were not even aware of the near tragedy of the day before. But there were those who were well aware of the incident; the hundreds without telephone service and the bridge operator who said, he simply didn't hear the ship's whistle.

During the late 1950's the United States government developed the Interstate Highway System to allow for high speed express travel on limited access roads. I-75, the multiple lane expressway, traverses north and south from the Canadian boarder at Sault St. Marie, Michigan over one thousand six hundred miles to Miami, Florida.

A person could conceivably drive from one of the most northern points in the United States to one of the most southern without stopping.

A double leaf bascule bridge, or more commonly known as a draw bridge, was built to carry the I-75 highway traffic over the Saginaw River.

On October 5, 1967 a Great Lakes freighter carefully threaded its way along the Saginaw River from Lake Huron's Saginaw Bay. It navigated the curving river with its four bascule bridges and two railroad swing bridges. The ship discharged its cargo of limestone upriver and began its return voyage downriver to the open water of Lake Huron's Saginaw Bay.

As the ship approached the draw bridge at Zilwaukee, which carried the cars and trucks of I-75 over the river, the steering mechanism of the ship failed! The ship attempted to slow and stop but it just wasn't going to happen.

The vessel crashed into one of the columns supporting the southbound lanes of the I-75 expressway. The ship, traveling at a slow speed, received very little damage and fortunately the damage to the bridge was also minimal and the traffic was diverted from the southbound lanes for several days while the damage was analyzed and repaired. Massive traffic jams were reported on I-75 at the Saginaw River.

The Great Lakes freighter that struck the Zilwaukee Bridge… the *J.F. Schoellkopf Jr.*

*The* J.F. Schoellkopf Jr. *with it's prow under the Zilwaukee Bridge.*
*Courtesy of the State of Michigan Archive, Lansing, Michigan.*

# THE FISHING TUG SEARCHLIGHT

**T**he Brown brothers, Walter, Albert, George and Harvey, had been fishing, working, and playing on Lake Huron since they were children. They began their fishing career under the guidance of their father Levi, first in small boats, then larger sailboats and propeller fishing boats. On Sunday April 21, 1907, the brothers proudly arrived in the harbor with their new fishing tug, *Searchlight*.

The *Searchlight* had been fishing Saginaw Bay before the Brown brothers purchased her. The seven year old tug, 40-feet in length with a beam of 11-feet, was built by the G. Miskin Boat Yard of Saginaw, Michigan. She was built of wood and powered by a steam engine driving a single propeller.

Shortly after the *Searchlight* arrived, a spring storm lashed the lake and the brothers couldn't get out to lift the nets they set earlier. It wasn't until late in April before the weather cleared sufficiently to allow them to take their new steam tug out.

Captain Walter Brown, the Master of the *Searchlight* on her first trip, had in the past been employed by the Life Saving Service and was known as a competent and well respected seaman. Serving as mate

Searchlight -X

**25**

*No photographs of the* Searchlight *exist, but the Brown Brothers fishing tug was similar to this style of vessel. From the Tony Lang Collection.*

on the *Searchlights'* initial voyage in the Brown Brothers fleet, was brother Harvey Brown. Harvey, 30, had served in the Life Saving Service with his older brother and was no stranger to the lake.

Others on board the *Searchlight* that day were Merton Perkins, fireman, and James Lester was deckhand. Edward Coveau was the ship's engineer employed to oversee the vessel's steam engine and had accompanied the *Searchlight* from Bay City. The last crewmember was deckhand, Angus Murphy.

The brothers were eager to get to the nets with their new boat. They looked forward to a great season.

Since the nets had been out an extended period, they anticipated a large catch and decided another boat might be needed. They prepared to take along one of the Brown brothers' sailboats to retrieve the nets and hopefully, a sizable catch.

Captain Albert Brown had for the last ten years been the master of the Brown brothers' boats but on this first voyage of the *Searchlight* he let his brother, Walter, have the honor. James Lester was to crew on the sailboat but at the last moment it was decided that he should go aboard the *Searchlight* and deckhand Alex Connor, who was more experienced with sails, would go on the sailboat. The boats left the harbor en route to their fishing nets some 12 miles to the east in Lake Huron.

The two ships were engaged in lifting their nets all day until about 4:30 when the sailboat had reached its capacity and was going to head towards shore.

The *Searchlight* informed them that they would remain for a while and pull more nets. The brothers had outfitted their new boat with a small steam powered crane on the bow to lift the nets. The lifting engine was working perfectly and raising the full nets was going smoothly.

On the way in, the wind began to freshen. By the time the sailboat had tied up to the fishing dock in the harbor, the weather had taken a turn for the worse. Within two hours, the weather deteriorated to a full gale blowing from the northeast.

The *Searchlight* and its crew of six had completed lifting nets and began making their way towards the harbor in gale. While covering the 12 miles to the harbor, the vessel was battling seas which were increasing in size as the wind increased in velocity.

The lookout on the watchtower in the harbor was Surfman Durkee. His assignment was to scan the lake, watching for signs of trouble. Through the wind blown rain he observed the *Searchlight* about 2 miles northeast of the Harbor Beach lighthouse. He continued to watch the tug until 7:25 that evening when through darkness and the storm he could no longer see the ship. He used his glass to scan the horizon but still could not sight the vessel.

Surfman Durkee telephoned Captain Ferris at the Life Saving station to inform him that he could no longer find the fishing tug. Captain Ferris quickly assembled a crew and went out to look for the missing ship. They searched the storm tossed lake for several hours with no results.

*The lookout tower at the Harbor Beach harbor of refuge. From the Tony Lang Collection.*

Captain Reynolds of the harbor tug *Johnson* was called to aid the Life Saving crew in the search for the ship. The two boats searched for hours, using torches in the dark, but all that was found were three fish boxes.

The rescue boats with their exhausted and freezing crew returned to shore with a thick coat of ice which had built up on the vessels from the waves breaking over them throughout the night.

In the morning, the lifesavers in their large gasoline surfboat set out south to look for *Searchlight* survivors or the boat's wreckage. They searched fifteen to twenty miles and turned up a compass box, two buckets marked "*Searchlight*", the port and starboard siding boxes with the name "*Searchlight*"on them, some fish net boxes, and other small pieces of debris. No survivors, no bodies. Nothing to indicate the cause of the foundering or the final resting place of the *Searchlight* and its crew of six.

The Tug *Johnson* and other vessels continued to search the area where the *Searchlight* was presumed to have disappeared. They dragged the bottom in hopes of finding the wreck. A diver was brought in to search the bottom, but all was in vain. The 40-foot tug *Searchlight* was never to be seen again. It just disappeared!

The disappearance of the *Searchlight* with its crew was the talk of the town. Never before had the small port town of Harbor Beach suffered such a disaster, six men taken to their death by Lake Huron. Wives, children, mothers, fathers, brothers, and friends were left to grieve their loss. Levi Brown, father of two of those lost, was shattered. Albert Brown also took the loss of his brothers very hard. Out of respect to them, he vowed he would quit the lake and never fish again.

There were many theories presented as to the cause of the loss. Some suggested that the crew did not close the hatches on their return trip and the mounting seas broke over the vessel, quickly filling her, and she foundered. This thought was not given much credence since the crew was so experienced, a mistake like that was unthinkable.

Two weeks after the accident a life jacket, hat and broken boards were found south of the harbor and were thought to be from the *Searchlight*. The broken boards were strong thick boards broken across the grain, indicating that a tremendous force must have occurred to break such sturdy lumber. This produced the thought that the tug's boiler must have exploded.

Captain Ferris of the Life Saving station discounted this theory in that an explosion that close to shore would have been seen and heard by the surfman on duty in the watchtower or by the keepers in the lighthouse.

## Harbor Beach T

Harbor Beach, Michigan, Thursday, April 25. 1907

Harbor Beach is a Big Busy Town

# SIX MEN DROWNED

### Fish Tug "Searchlight" Goes Down With all Hands Two Miles Outside of Breakwater.

Four of The Crew of Six Were Harbor Beach Men.
Entire Town in State of Gloom. Worst
Disaster in History of Town.

was pretty tired so went home and went to bed early. This morning several people came to the house and asked if I was there and finally I was told about the wreck. I'm all unnerved today. It was terrible."

Of the crew of six who met their death on the "Searchlight", four were residents of this place, all having lived here practically all their lives. Engineer Coveau of Bay City, and Deckhand Murray of Detroit, were strangers and little or nothing can be learned about them. The engineer came with the tug which arrived Sunday and beyond the fact that he had a family in Bay City, nothing can be found out regarding him. Deckhand Angus Murray came here from Detroit a short time ago and has one sister living in Detroit.

*The headline of the April 25, 1907* Harbor Beach Times.

Captain Ferris's explanation was that the boards must have been broken by the extreme forces the vessel was subjected to while it was sent to the bottom. The steam net lifter, which weighed about a half of a ton, and the steam boilers and engine, would be violently torn from their mountings thus easily breaking thick boards in the process.

Captain Albert Brown disagreed with all previous theories and presented his own. He felt that since his brother was coming in from the northeast, the tug was taking the seas broadside. A vessel with a full, heavy load does not respond to the action of the waves quickly. It rolls sluggishly in the waves. And the heavy net lifter on the bow made the vessel top heavy, increasing its propensity to roll. Captain Albert theorized that the *Searchlight* took a large wave broadside and rolled to port; before it could recover another wave struck it and turned the tug over. That would explain why the experienced seamen on the *Searchlight* did not signal the Life Savers; they had no time to do so. It would explain why the raft on the vessel was not found; it was still lashed to the ship. There was no time for the men to use it. The men apparently were not prepared for whatever happened to the *Searchlight*. They could not jump off the stricken craft since they must have been inside the tug when its fate materialized, explaining why no bodies were recovered.

Despite the fact that the *Searchlight* was close to the harbor of refuge, within sight of the Life Saving station, the wreckage of the vessel or bodies of the crew were never found!

About 10 days after the disappearance of the *Searchlight* a bottle was found floating near a Lexington, Michigan beach, some 45 miles to the south. In the bottle was a note, it read;

"April 22"
"*Searchlight* turned turtle off Harbor Beach, going down, except Jack in cork jacket."

M. Perkins

Superintendent of the Life Saving Service, Captain J.G. Kiah, who received the note from the finder, stated that although the date is incorrect he believed the note to be original. Others questioned the validly of the note because it was felt no time existed for Mr. Perkins to write such a note. The note was passed on to relatives to verify the handwriting but they could not determine if it was genuine. It never was determined.

The mystery surrounding the disappearance of the *Searchlight* resurfaced again six and a half years later. The wreck of the *Searchlight* was again on the front page of the newspaper.

On November 9-11, 1913, what experienced sailors call the most turbulent storm that ever laid siege on Lake Huron assaulted the Great Lakes. Huge, modern, steel ships went missing on the lake, while many others were severely damaged. Hundreds of sailors were carried to their deaths as their ships sank to the bottom.

On November 11, 1913 a fisherman from the village of White Rock, Michigan, 12 miles south of Harbor Beach reported finding the smokestack and parts of the cabin from a fishing tug. Near the debris was

# BODY ON BEACH BELIEVED TUG SEARCHLIGHT VICTIM

MARINE MYSTERY AT HARBOR BEACH MAY BE SOLVED. PART OF BOAT'S SMOKE STACK IDENTIFIED BY FISHERMEN. BODY AND PARTS OF WRECK WASHED UP BY SUNDAY'S STORM.

found a badly decomposed body. Fishermen, who should know, recognized it as the cabin and smokestack of the missing tug *Searchlight*.

The cause of the disappearance of the Brown brothers fishing tug *Searchlight* and its final resting place is still a mystery. Did the tug explode? Did it plunge bow first to the bottom? Or did it, as Captain Albert Brown suggested, turn turtle, fill with water and sink? To this day it remains one of Lake Huron's mysteries.

# THE JINX OF CAPTAIN WALTER NEAL

S ailors of yesterday were a superstitious lot. They avoided ships if they were launched on Friday the Thirteenth, if a workman was killed during its construction, if the vessel had been involved in a previous accident involving death, sometimes even if a woman was onboard, and for many other reasons the ship would be considered unlucky. While the superstitious thoughts are not shared by all Great Lakes sailors, one man who questioned the existence of a jinx was Captain Walter Neal.

Life in the wilds of Michigan's Upper Peninsula was meant only for the stoutest of souls. Daniel Parish was one such man who made his living in the Upper Peninsula.

Dan Parish labored in the woods as a trapper and hunter and during the winters he took on the job of mail carrier. He delivered the mail by dog sled, from Sault Ste. Marie to the lumbering camps and villages around Whitefish Bay.

On one March day in 1920, while delivering the mail, Dan came upon an eerie sight. Not believing what he saw he slowed the dogs and wiped his eyes; not too far from the lake was a man in the winter woods. The man just stood there, not moving. He was frozen in place!

*A photograph of the dog sled mail carriers from Sault Ste. Marie. From the Bayliss Public Library, Sault Ste. Marie, Michigan.*

Suspecting the frozen body might be that of a sailor from a shipwreck, Dan crawled over the ice flows at the shore of Lake Superior and found an ice encrusted lifeboat... and more bodies, frozen in an icy tomb.

Eight of the crew of 17 from the doomed steamer *Myron* had been found. The frozen bodies of the sailors had been there since their ship had gone down over four months earlier.

The *Myron*, built in 1888 as a lumber hooker, had departed from Lake Superior's Munising, Michigan on November 21, 1919. She had a load of lumber bound for Buffalo, New York on the extreme eastern end of Lake Erie. The 186-foot *Myron* was teamed up with the barge *Miztec* in tow. The *Miztec* was also with a full load of lumber.

The ship and her barge steamed out of Munising Bay, through the narrow pass between Sand Point and Grand Island, where so many ships had stranded, and out into the open water of Lake Superior. While en route, a storm struck the lake; a storm that was unusually strong, even for Lake Superior in November.

The small steamer and the barge *Miztec* battled the high winds and towering seas the lake threw at them. About 80 miles into the trip Captain Walter Neal, Master of the *Myron*, knew they were in trouble. His ship was being pounded relentlessly.

Another larger steamer, the 480-foot *Adriatic*, came next to the smaller *Myron*, staying to windward, in effect blocking the wind and seas for the smaller vessel.

The ships traveled in this manner trying to make the shelter offered behind Whitefish Point. The conditions were terrible and the steamer was in a bad way. The *Myron* was taking on water and so far the pumps were keeping it at bay, but the strain of towing the *Miztec* behind her was hampering and even threatening the *Myron's* very existence.

Captain Neal had to make a decision; he ordered the towline cut. The *Miztec*, and its crew, would have to fend for herself.

The 194-foot barge *Miztec* was originally built as a two-mast schooner but as so many other Great Lake schooners, she had been converted to a barge, destined to serve out her career towed behind a steam-powered ship.

The sailors on the barge were able to raise some sails, tattered from lack of use, and through the Grace of God made it behind Whitefish Point and dropped anchor. The crew of the *Miztec* hoped and prayed their 39-year-old vessel would hold together in the storm long enough for them to be rescued.

The *Myron* and *Adriatic* made it to the shelter of the peninsula but the *Myron* was in rough shape. The ship had taken a pounding at the hands of the vicious lake and the ship was taking on water at an alarming rate. The pumps discharged water but not enough.

The water rose in the engine room until it extinguished the fire. No fire, no steam. No steam, no propulsion or steering, and no pumps! The *Myron* was in a helpless state. Captain Neal ordered the men to abandon ship.

The *Adriatic* attempted to rescue the *Myron's* crew. Twice she struck the bottom while trying to save the men, but the violent storm eventually turned her away.

The crew abandoned the ship but Captain Neal chose to stay with the *Myron*. He was going to try to ride it out with the vessel that brought him this far, although he knew it might mean his death.

Waves assaulting the ship washed the cargo of lumber off the deck of the *Myron*. The lake was covered with lengths of cut lumber; many splintered, slammed into the lifeboats and tore holes in them, casting the crew into the frigid lake. The men swam as they might, but the storm-tossed wood boards crushed many of them. Those who were lucky enough to make it to shore froze to death.

As the *Myron* broke apart, Captain Neal found himself in the tumultuous sea. He swam towards what remained of the pilothouse, and crawled onto the debris as it was thrown about by the violent waves… he held on for his life.

The *Adriatic* saw the captain but the big boat couldn't get close enough to rescue him.

Another ship, the *H.P. Macintos*, was able to get to within 15-feet of the captain, but they were unable to save him. They shouted over the raging storm and crashing waves that they would send a small boat for him… but they never did. The ship departed the area leaving the captain to a certain death.

The captain clung to his makeshift raft while the waves broke and sent wind blown spray, stinging his face and hands. The cold of a snowy fall Lake Superior storm ebbed his energy and snow piled up on his wet body. Numb with cold, he held onto the remains of the pilothouse a horrendous 20 hours before he was rescued.

Captain Walter Neal was the sole survivor of the sinking of the *Myron*. But the barge *Miztec* and her crew lived to sail another day. The *Miztec* was repaired and put back into service. Captain Neal was healed and soon went back to sea.

On July 18, 1920, the Steamer *Charles H. Bradley* was towing two barges, one of them, the *Mary Woolson*. While traveling up Lake Huron they encountered a storm off Thunder Bay. The *Bradley* struggled, towing the two barges through the high seas and finally lowered anchor to ride out the storm.

While anchored, the *Bradley* was rammed from behind by the barge *Mary Woolson*. The *Mary Woolson* sank and the *Bradley* was badly damaged. The complete story of the incident can be found in this book in the *Charles H. Bradley* chapter. The second of the two barges went aground but was not badly damaged. It was the barge *Miztec*. The captain of the barges on that trip… Captain Walter Neal.

On May 14, 1921 the 202-foot wood steamer *Zillah* was towing two barges on Lake Superior. The *Zillah* and one of the barges were going to Munising. The other barge was headed for Superior, Wisconsin. A spring storm was unleashing its fury on the lake with cold, snow, wind and waves.

At 3:00 in the morning, the vessels passed Whitefish Point but after they rounded the peninsula they received the full brunt of the storm. The steamer's captain chose to come about and shelter in the protected waters of Whitefish Bay.

Coming about in the heavy seas with two barges in tow was not an easy feat but they were successful. While returning to the safety behind Whitefish Point, the towline snapped. There was nothing the *Zillah* could do in the weather conditions, the barges were on their own. The barge

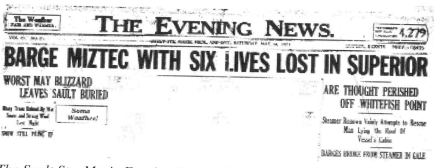

*The Sault Ste. Marie Evening News, tells of the tragedy which befell the barge* Miztec.

*Peshtigo*, traveling light, quickly lowered her anchor. The anchors held fast and she was able to ride out the storm.

The *Peshtigo* sustained heavy damage. The wheelhouse was destroyed beyond repair; her steering mechanism was destroyed, the wheel almost torn through the wheelhouse.

The second barge, with her seven man and one woman crew, was not so lucky; they drifted with the wild wind and pounding seas. The barge was tossed about by the waves. The crew, unable to hold a course in the turbulent seas, knew their lives were in peril.

No one knows what happened to that second barge; the snow was so dense that nobody saw, and the crew didn't live through the experience to tell. All that is known is that the *Zillah's* second barge was destroyed and sunk to the bottom of the area seasoned sailors call the "Graveyard of the Lakes."

All six men and the one woman, the sister-in-law of the Zillah's captain, were killed when the barge apparently broke up in the storm. It sank just a few miles from the location where the *Myron* had gone to bottom just months before.

The name of the barge that sunk to the bottom… the *Miztec*. The first mate that day on the *Zillah*… Captain Walter Neal.

"All of my mishaps at sea have been connected to the *Miztec*,"Captain Neal said. "She has been a Jonah to me, and I guess I have been to her."

Captain Neal said he believes the jinx of the *Miztec* has finally been broken.

# THE CAPTAIN'S AUNT

**T**he *New Connecticut* was a schooner that sailed the Great Lakes in the early 1800's. Her Captain and owner was Captain Gilman Appleby of Conneaut, Ohio.

In 1833 the Captain's aunt had been visiting from Buffalo, New York and was ready to return. The captain tried to persuade her to stay a while longer until he would have an opportunity to take her home himself. He was busy at the time overseeing the construction of his new steamboat. She had her mind made up and she was ready to return home. His schooner *New Connecticut* was departing for Buffalo in short order so Captain Appleby took his aunt to the ship.

It was a little over 100 miles from Conneaut to Buffalo, but about 30 miles into the trip the schooner ran into weather. A squall developed with winds of surprising velocity. The schooner, with full sails flying, was surprised by the sudden squall and heeled to as the wind bore down on her. Unable to recover the vessel rolled over on her side.

Lake water poured in through all openings, flooding the cargo hold and cabins.

The crew could not get to the cabins but they were sure since the squall appeared so fast and the ship rolled so quickly anyone caught below had surely drowned. To save

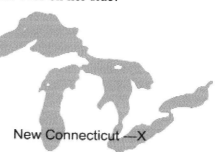

New Connecticut —X

**39**

themselves, they had to take to the yawl before the *New Connecticut* slipped below the waves.

The crew pulled at the oars through the wind and waves towards shore. They reported the accident and news made it back to Captain Appleby in Conneaut that his ship had capsized and was feared to be lost. Also his aunt had been trapped in her cabin and drowned.

Captain Appleby was distraught over the loss of his aunt. He felt guilty; he should have insisted she wait until he could have taken her to Buffalo personally.

Three days after the accident Captain Appleby contacted the steamer, *William Peacock*, and asked the master to keep an eye out for the *New Connecticut*. She might still be afloat and Captain Appleby felt obligated to retrieve his aunt's body and take it to Buffalo for a proper burial.

The *Peacock* spotted the wood *New Connecticut* still afloat. The steamer came abreast the capsized schooner and men armed with poles boarded the schooner. The men rammed the poles through the wood hull into the interior of the vessel. If they hit something that felt like a body they would make a bigger hole and retrieve the body. Despite several holes in the hull, the body of Captain Appleby's aunt was not found. They figured her body had probably been washed out of the hull and sunk to the bottom of Lake Erie. The search was terminated and the *William Peacock* went on her way.

When Captain Appleby received information that the *New Connecticut* was still afloat but that the *Peacock* had failed to find any bodies aboard, he was determined to find the floating wreck.

The captain set off with a vessel equipped to right the *New Connecticut* since she was still floating. The ship combed the area of Lake Erie near where the *Peacock* found the capsized schooner until it was located still afloat... five days after the schooner had capsized!

With much effort the *New Connecticut* was righted. The plan was to right the ship, put the pumps to her, and tow her to the nearest harbor for repairs. Since she was still afloat the vessel could be repaired and put back into service. Possibly, once righted, Captain Appleby could find the body of his aunt.

As she was righted, water poured out of the cabins, the decks were awash and the crew scrambled aboard the schooner. The men dragged pumps onboard the *New Connecticut* to empty her for her journey back to shore. The men, busy with their tasks, stopped dead in their tracks as a cabin door opened and Captain Appleby's aunt appeared... she was standing in the passageway...she was alive!

Shaken, suffering from hypothermia and pale from fear, she stepped out on the deck on weary legs and collapsed.

Comforted by her nephew and her son, she told her tale of horror as the ship rolled over trapping her in the cabin and how she had heard the crew preparing to leave the vessel but despite her screams they didn't hear her.

The *New Connecticut* rolled in the heavy seas and water rose slowly in the cabin until it was waist deep. She screamed to the crew of the *Peacock* but they didn't hear either. In their efforts to locate her body by ramming poles through the hull they almost speared her. She yelled to her rescuers asking if she should grab the pole to be pulled free, but they didn't hear. They departed the capsized vessel not hearing her pleas for help.

For the five days and nights she was trapped, the water continued to rise in the cabin. Standing in water up to her armpits, she couldn't sit or lay down, she slept standing for brief moments. Her only nourishment was a single cracker and an onion that floated by.

After her harrowing experience aboard the *New Connecticut*, the captain's aunt was definitely ready to get to the safety and security of her home in Buffalo.

# ACCIDENT AT THE SOO LOCKS

**A** ridge of red sandstone runs along the southeastern end of Lake Superior. The sandstone holds back Lake Superior to a level 21-feet higher than the level of Lake Huron. Because of this height difference, the water from Lake Superior pours into the St. Marys River (the connecting waterway between Superior and Lake Huron) at a speed

*An aerial view of the locks at Sault Ste. Marie. Canada is on the right and United States on the left. From the collections of the Michigan Archives, Lansing, Michigan.*

---Sault Ste. Marie

of 24 miles per hour creating a rapids. The rapids made it impossible for all but canoes navigated by skillful Native Americans to pass through.

For a ship to move south from Lake Superior to the lower Great Lakes or north into Lake Superior a lock would need to be constructed. A lock is a man made structure to raise or lower a vessel according to the lake levels.

To lower a ship from Lake Superior to the level of the St. Marys River, the following steps are taken:

1. The south lock gates are closed.
2. The downbound ship enters the lock.
3. The north gates close behind the ship.
4. Valves are opened at the bottom of the lock allowing water in the lock to flow into the St. Marys River.
5. Once lowered to the level of the St. Marys River the south gate opens and the ship leaves the lock.

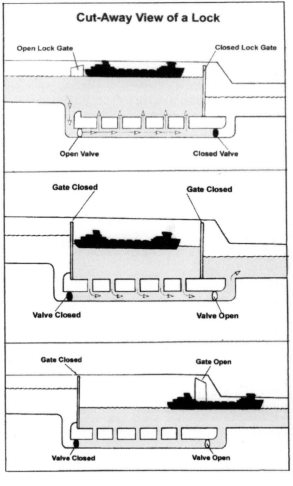

**Cut-Away View of a Lock**

Open Lock Gate

Closed Lock Gate

Open Valve

Closed Valve

Gate Closed

Gate Closed

Valve Closed

Valve Open

Gate Closed

Gate Open

Valve Closed

Valve Open

*A Great Lakes freighter,* Carl D. Bradley, *awaits the massive lock gates to open to continue on its course into Lake Superior. From the collections of the Michigan Archives, Lansing, Michigan.*

To raise a ship up to the level of Lake Superior the process is reversed.

By the mid 1700s, fur trappers were attracted to the Lake Superior area by the abundance of wildlife. The animals trapped were stripped of their pelts in the forests and the valuable fur pelts were taken by canoe to Sault Ste. Marie where they were carried around the rapids and packed aboard larger ships to be transported to Europe.

In 1797 the first lock was constructed to allow canoes to be lowered from the height of Lake Superior down the 21-feet to the level of the St. Marys River. The lock was 30-feet long by less than 9-feet wide.

The Lake Superior region was overflowing with nature's bounty. In addition to its wildlife, the area is rich in lumber and minerals such as copper and iron ore. As demand for these riches increased in the cities of the lower lakes, the need for larger ships to transport the cargo and a set of locks at the Soo (The nickname given to the Sault Ste. Marie area.) needed to be built which would be large enough for the vessels to pass through.

In 1853 the State of Michigan began work on the Harvey locks. The Harvey consisted to two locks, each 350-feet long and 70-feet wide. The ships passing up through the locks would be raised 10-feet in the first lock and another 10-feet in the second up to the level of Lake Superior.

As the size of vessels increased, larger locks were constructed on both the Canadian and American sides of the river. The multiple locks at Sault Ste. Marie were one of the busiest waterways on the lakes with cargos of lumber, iron ore and copper shipped south to the growing cities on Lakes Huron, Michigan, Erie and Ontario.

Most shipping traffic passes through the locks without incident, but on June 9, 1909 that wasn't the case.

On that day the Canadian Pacific Railroad's passenger ship *Assinboia* was preparing to lock through the Canadian Lock from Lake Superior.

The ship was tied up at the approach waiting for the lock chamber to fill to the level of Lake Superior. Once the level was attained the giant gates opened and the passenger ship passed into the chamber.

It was a warm late spring day. The sun was high in the blue sky and the passengers lined the decks eager to experience their ship lowered the 21-feet to the level of the St. Marys River.

The crew was busy on the deck. They would need to loosen the ship's lines that held the *Assinboia* to the lock walls as the emptying valve was opened and the ship descended.

Once the *Assinboia* was secured in the chamber, the Pittsburgh Steel Company's freighter *Crescent City* was easing its way into the chamber to pass through with the passenger ship.

At the same time approaching the Canadian lock from the south was the Gilchrist steamer *Perry G. Walker*. The intent of the *Walker* was to tie up to the southern approach of the lock to await the down-bound ships to lock through, then enter the lock and continue it's up-bound trip.

The upper lock gates were open as the *Crescent City* entered the chamber. All of the force of Lake Superior was held back only by the south gate of the lock.

As the *Walker* approached from the south to tie up at the lock approach, Captain Mosher felt they were going too fast and called for the engineer to slow the ship. The ship didn't slow. More calls to the engineer were made, and still the captain's orders went unheeded. The *Perry G. Walker* continued towards the lock gate, ramming it.

The impact, combined with the millions of pounds of pressure exerted on the gates from Lake Superior, resulted in the gates breaking. One gate

*The beautiful Canadian passenger ship* Assinboia. *From the collections of the Michigan Archives, Lansing, Michigan.*

was washed away in the torrent of water that flowed through the open north gate and out of the lock chamber. The mooring lines of the *Assinboia* snapped like strings as the passenger ship was torn from the lock wall and began an uncontrollable passage through the locks. Witnesses said the big passenger ship nosed down with her rudder and wheel exposed. Somehow she missed the *Walker* as she surfed by.

The steamer *Crescent City* was not yet tied up in the lock chamber and she was shot forward on the force of the water rushing through the lock at an estimated 40 miles per hour.

The *Crescent City* smashed into the *Assinboia* as she was sent by the passenger ship, rammed the lock gate and then struck the *Walker* on her wild ride through the Canadian Lock.

The swift moving river carried the *Assinboia*, grounding on a bank at the lower approach. Listing to starboard, she was later pulled off of the bank by a tug.

The *Crescent City* was badly damaged and made its way to the Fort Brady dock. She was taking on water and slowly sinking.

The *Perry G. Walker* was forced backwards by the torrent of water pouring through the lock, the approach slamming into the *Assinboia*. The

*Lake Superior flows through the damaged south gate of the Canadian lock. From the collections of the Michigan Archives, Lansing, Michigan.*

anchor of the passenger ship smashed a hole in the wood hull of the *Walker*. Fortunately for the *Walker*, the hole was above the waterline.

A smaller vessel loaded with passengers coming from Lake Superior, unaware of the accident, entered the approach to the lock. The tremendous current rushing through the lock chamber caught the boat attempting to pull it through the lock. The boat, struggling against the ripping current, was able to back out of harms way and avoid almost certain destruction.

A temporary patch was put over the hole in the *Perry G. Walker* which was caused by the *Walker* striking the *Assinboia* anchor. After a couple of days the *Walker* was permitted to continue north.

The *Assinboia* was listing, not due to taking on water but because its cargo had shifted. A diver was called to inspect the bottom and found all to be okay. The cargo was readjusted and the ship headed south along the river. The next day it was reported at the Soo that the *Assinboia* had sunk by DeTour Island. It was an unfounded rumor.

The *Crescent City* received the most damage of the three ships involved. A patch was installed over a hole on her port bow and

*The torrent of water flowing through the Canadian Lock. From the Bayliss Public Library.*

compressors were activated to pump water out of the ship. But with the weight of a full load of iron ore the ship sank to the bottom at the dock.

The ships were repaired and continue to sail the Lakes. The flow of water through the damaged lock gate was stopped through the use of a temporary dam and the gates were repaired. Lock experts from the

*Whenever there was an accident at the Soo Locks the steamer traffic was backed up. As can be seen in the photograph. From the State of Michigan Archives, Lansing, Michigan.*

Panama Canal went to the Soo to study the accident to make sure a similar incident did not occur at those locks. But, on a positive side, Captain Rice, of the steamer *Crescent City*, claimed that he held the record for the fastest lockage through the Soo Locks!

*(Authors Note: The Soo Locks are a must see for any lover of maritime history and commercial ship traffic on the Great Lakes. Located on the St. Marys River at Sault Ste. Marie, Michigan on the south side and Sault Ste. Marie, Ontario on the north, the observer can watch ships raise or lower 21-feet as they travel through the locks, tour a Great Lakes Freighter, visit great museums on each side of the river. It is well worth the trip.)*

# E.M. FORD SANK LIKE A ROCK

**I**n 1979 the *E.M. Ford* had reached the ripe old age of 81 years. For a Great Lakes freighter battling 81 seasons of storm tossed waves, early spring ice and millions of tons of cargo poured into and taken out of her hold, that is pretty darn good.

The *E.M. Ford* was built in 1898 for the Cleveland Cliffs Company as the steamer Presque Isle. She sailed with the company until 1955 when she was sold. After modifications, the 428-foot ship was re-christened the *E.M. Ford.*

On the evening of December 25, 1979 a storm bore down on Lake Michigan with 15- to 20-foot seas. While not pleasant for the crew, the *E.M. Ford* could handle it. Over her career she had seen worse storms. Unfortunately for the ship, she was not out on the open lake where she could ride out the storm. She was moored at the Jones Island dock at Milwaukee, Wisconsin.

On that Christmas day on 1979, the *E.M. Ford* was tied up to a dock. The ship had arrived two days prior with 7,000 tons of cargo from Alpena, Michigan. Because of the holiday, the cargo was not scheduled to be unloaded until later in the week and

X---- E.M. Ford

*The* E.M. Ford. *From the Great Lakes Photographic Collection of Hugh Clark.*

most of the crew of 30 departed to spend Christmas with their families. Only five men stayed behind to keep watch aboard the docked ship.

The winds blew ferociously up to 60 miles per hour. The *Ford* was rolled at the dock under the force of the wind until one at a time the 16 mooring lines, made up from 4-1/2 inch nylon rope and 1 inch steel cable, snapped under the stress. The big ship then was shoved around by the wind.

The *E.M. Ford* smashed into the dock repeatedly, crashing against the sturdy steel covered concrete structure. The five men onboard made a frantic call for help. They were afraid the ship would be beaten into pieces, taking them along with it. A tugboat came to their assistance, maneuvered close and removed the crew, but the wind and waves continued to smash the ship against the dock.

Attempts were made to secure the *Ford*. Cables were made fast to the ship and winches were used to pull it away from the dock wall. More cables were added to stabilize the vessel but the damage had been done.

While the ship was repeatedly pounded against the dock, a 24-foot gash was torn in the ship's starboard bow. Along the port side cracks appeared in the hull, some up to 12-feet long.

The ship began taking on water. Slowly the *E.M. Ford* settled. When the storm subsided, the freighter was found lying on the bottom.

An initial examination revealed that water had entered the engine room. The gashes in the hull would need to be temporarily repaired and much of the water pumped out before the *Ford* could be moved to a dry dock for permanent repairs.

# E.M. FORD SANK LIKE A ROCK

*The* E.M. Ford *lies on the bottom of Jones Island dock at Milwaukee after being beaten against the dock by the December 25, 1979 storm. The* E.M. Ford *was eventually raised and still is used on the Great Lakes. Photo by Norbert Huskins,* E.M. Ford *Chief Engineer. Provided by David Huskins.*

Once the ship had been raised it was discovered that water had seeped into the cargo hold and that the ship's cargo had become wet. The *E.M. Ford's* cargo of 7,000 tons of dry cement had crusted over. A three foot thick crust of cement had formed in the cargo hold!

Before the ship could be repaired several tons of hardened cement had to be broken out with jack hammers. The process took weeks.

Ironically, the ship that sunk and became the butt of many jokes; "The Concrete Freighter", "The Cement Mixer", "The ship that floats like a rock", is still afloat.

The *E.M. Ford* holds the distinction of being the oldest ship still operating on the Great Lakes. The *E.M. Ford* is at this writing tied up in the Saginaw River for use as a floating cement storage container at 108 years old!

# THE SCHOONER WILLIAM R. HANNA SAILS BY THE HARBOR

**O**n Saturday November 6, 1880, the *William R. Hanna* was downbound on Lake Huron. What started as just another day for a Great Lakes sailor, ended as a day Captain Bedford and his crew would never forget.

Six days earlier, the schooner *Hanna* left Port Huron with a cargo of supplies for Prentiss Bay, some 240 miles to the north. There they exchanged their cargo for 1,600 tamarack railroad ties assigned for Toledo.

John Susa, a deckhand on the *Hanna,* reported to Captain Bedford that the railroad ties were extremely heavy. Upon inspection the Captain found them to be waterlogged. This concerned the crew, for the heavy railroad ties stacked on the deck would make the ship top heavy and prone to roll in a sea, but Captain Bedford, seemingly unconcerned, ordered the men to continue the loading.

On Friday at 2:00 pm the *Hanna* cleared port. Before long they were under full sail with a light wind, bound south on northern Lake Huron. Several hours later as they passed Thunder Bay Island, the weather changed a bit. It started to snow and the wind shifted out of the northeast.

The *Hanna* continued south, the weather nothing

X---William R. Hanna

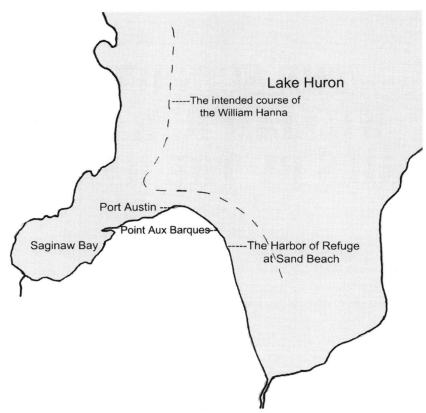

Lake Huron

-----The intended course of
the William Hanna

Port Austin ---

Point Aux Barques

Saginaw Bay

-----The Harbor of Refuge
at Sand Beach

worse than she had encountered on previous trips. The crew made preparations to cross Saginaw Bay. Captain Bedford followed his usual course, sailing south and slightly west into the bay towards Port Austin, then changing course to the southeast, sailing out into the lake to clear the dangerous reefs near the Point aux Barques lighthouse.

On this trip, as the ship entered Saginaw Bay, the storm increased in intensity, quickly blowing into a gale with blinding snow out of the northeast. The wind blew furiously and the old ship's canvas being no match, ripped the ship's jib to tatters. The crew fought to lower the main sail, but it was a slow process. The velocity of the wind hampering their every move, they continued on sailing under the foresail and staysail.

Through the blizzard, one of the crew spotted the light of the Port Austin Reef lighthouse. A crewman asked if they might seek shelter at Port Austin, not wishing to continue in the storm. Captain Bedford knew the narrow, shallow entrance to Port Austin was a challenge to enter in clear weather; he did not want to chance losing his vessel on the rocky reefs. As he had so many times before, Captain Bedford ordered the ship to turn south by east to pass above Point aux Barques and out into the lake. Unfortunately, this course would put the vessel in the trough of the waves.

The *Hanna* rolled in the seas as it entered Lake Huron. Now on a south-by-east course, the beacon of the Point aux Barques light station could be seen off her starboard beam. The sailors watched the light, when they could see it through the snow, hoping the sea would be kind to them and allow them to make the government harbor of refuge at Sand Beach (presently named Harbor Beach).

The pounding the vessel had endured over its career might have caused it, or maybe the years of cargo loading, shifting and unloading caused it, or possibly it was an undiscovered weakness, but the *Hanna* split a seam below the water line and began taking on water.

One of the deckhands found water in the hull. Captain Bedford ordered the crew to the pumps. Down in the bowels of a ship rolling and pitching in the seas the men labored at the pumps, until they realized that she was filling faster than the pumps were emptying. Their efforts were futile.

The captain and crew turned their attention to survival. They steered for the safety offered at the harbor at Sand Beach. They prayed the ship would stay afloat and in one piece until they reached the harbor.

About five miles northeast of Sand Beach, the *Hanna's* mate, Sylvester Ray, was standing near the wheelsman, while the Captain and Ralph Finelson were forward checking the sails. Suddenly, the combination of the ship rolling in the trough of the waves, the overly heavy deck load of water soaked railroad ties, and the gale force winds won the battle; the ship broached and rolled onto its side. The two men at the wheel jumped for the rail and hung on.

The Captain and Finelson, forward, were thrown into the cold water of the lake. Fortunately, they were close enough to the rigging lying along the surface that they were able to grasp and hold it. Slowly the two stunned and freezing men climbed along the rigging onto the hull of the ship.

The *Hanna*, lying on her side in night's darkness, in a blizzard, was pushed south/southeast by the raging wind and waves. With each wave crashing on the ship and the spray covering the men clinging to anything that offered security, the men prayed for rescue and comforted each other. The crew watched over the captain, an older man, who was suffering terribly from exposure.

Sometime that evening, one of the men saw lights not too far from them, maybe 500 yards. The snow momentarily let up and the almost frozen men realized the ship was drifting by the harbor of refuge at Sand Beach, blown by the ferocious wind.

They yelled out, screamed into the night for help. They could see lights and men moving about the breakwater but no assistance came to them. They had not been seen or heard.

The wind shifted around from the northwest and fearing they would be driven out into the lake, Sylvester Ray crawled forward along the side of the cabin, supporting himself on the mast, finally reaching the bow. With numb hands he pulled his knife, cut away the weather strapping and let go the anchors. He didn't know if this would help or not, but if they continued as they were, they probably wouldn't be seen again until their frozen bodies floated up on a Canadian beach.

The anchor and all of her chain noisily played out and dragged along the bottom. Suddenly the anchors grabbed, the ship jerked and the *Hanna* righted! The men tumbled from the side of the cabin onto the deck, and on hands and knees they crawled to the rail.

The ship was upright but now the crew had another problem. The waves were breaking amidship washing the deck in a freezing waterfall. The waves striking the cabin ripped it from the deck and washed it away. The crew, now all but dead from their ordeal, found a four foot by ten foot area on the foredeck which was sheltered from the waves and spray. The crew gathered there trying to stay out of the bone chilling lake spray, huddled, trying to keep warm.

The younger men fared better than the captain, who became paralyzed with cold. The men knew the captain would not live through the night unless they walked him in the small dry area to keep his blood flowing.

The men slipped in and out of a cold fretful sleep through the night. At day's first light, they shook the snow from their bodies and looked to shore for assistance. The blizzard continued and no one from shore or from the scores of ships tied to the breakwater could see the *Hanna*.

About 10:00 am, almost 12 hours after their ship had been blown over, the snow let up and the wind slowed. The crew of the *Hanna* found themselves riding in high seas, almost on the reef off the south of the harbor.

The propeller steamer *L. Worthington* had sought the government harbor when the skies turned gray and the winds and snow approached. The ship spent the night tied to the breakwater, the waves crashing on the wood superstructure, the spray covering the ship in a blanket of ice.

*Ships sheltering at the government harbor of refuge at Sand Beach, Michigan. From the David Busch Collection.*

During the night, Captain St. Clair of the *Worthington* awoke and was walking the deck while the storm threatened his ship, even as it lay secured in the harbor. At one point the captain thought he heard something. He walked out on the bridge, looked out into the lake, obscured by the weather. He heard it again, it sounded like men out on the lake screaming for help.

Bothered by the pained cries, Captain St. Clair could not sleep the rest of the night. He kept looking out into the storm for the source of the cries. He was thinking of the men possibly dying nearby, but there was nothing he could do.

At morning's light, the snow still prevented him from seeing anything on the lake. Later when the snow slowed he peered out into the lake and was startled to see a ship at anchor, just below the south breakwater. The ship, missing much of its deck work and its rigging in disarray, was being ravaged by the waves.

In the year 1880 there wasn't a Life Saving Station at Sand Beach to go to the assistance of the *Hanna*. Any rescue would need to come from the ships in the harbor. At once, the *Worthington* made ready to go to their assistance.

The *Worthington* steamed out of the harbor, Captain St. Clair racked with guilt for not doing anything when he first heard the cries of the sailors. Knowing the water to be shallow and made shallower by the rise and fall of the waves, the *Worthington* slowly made way toward the *Hanna*. The captain searched the vessel for signs of life, but there weren't any.

The wheelsman of the *Worthington* skillfully maneuvered his vessel, trying to come along side the *Hanna*. As they neared the *Hanna*, the ship rolling in the waves beat against the hull of the Steamer forcing her to back off. But Captain St. Clair was relieved to see movement from the bodies lying on the *Hanna's* deck.

Another attempt at rescue was made with the same results. Captain St. Clair then ordered his ship to the lee of the *Hanna*, a move he had previously rejected, fearing the shallow water. Slowly inching forward, with a watchman at the bow, the *Worthington* came close enough for a man to jump to the *Hanna*. He quickly helped the crew, benumbed by their harrowing night on the lake, to the safety of the *Worthington*. Captain Bedford, paralyzed with cold was last off his ship.

The following day the seas had subsided and the steam tug Jessie went to the *Hanna* to pull her off the reef. With fresh men at the pumps, enough water was removed and the *Hanna* reluctantly gave up her hold on the bottom and floated free. She was pulled the short distance into the harbor, anchored and awaited repairs.

After a doctor saw the sailors and administered restoratives, they slowly recovered from their night on the lake. Captain Bedford, after days of rest, went to his ship to survey the damage. It was repairable. Unfortunately, days later another fall storm came from the northeast, ripping the *Hanna* from its anchor and driving it ashore. The *William R. Hanna* was severely damaged and declared a total loss. It was a total loss for Captain Bedford who had just before this fateful trip, bought out his partner's half share, making the *William R. Hanna* all his.

But Captain Bedford and his crew would long remember their trip huddled together through a blinding snowstorm, passing by the harbor of refuge on the port side of the capsized schooner *Hanna*.

# GERMAN SUBMARINE IN THE GREAT LAKES!

**O**n June 7, 1921 a large freighter departed Gary, Indiana after discharging its load of iron ore at a steel mill. The ship headed out into Lake Michigan towards its next destination, its next cargo. About 50 miles into its trip the captain looked out the port side of the wheelhouse. He stared in disbelief. It was a German Submarine! The captain ordered half speed.

On that morning, the 185-foot German submarine *UC-97* stealthily rode along the surface of the waters of Lake Michigan, in the heartland of the United States. The vessel was moving slowly yet it was capable of 11.5 knots on the surface and 6.6 submerged. The submarine was equipped with three 20-inch torpedo tubes, a 3.4 inch gun, 6 mine tubes and could carry 14 mines. The ship was a veritable war machine.

Also on that day, the 265-foot Naval Reserve ship, *S.S. Wilmette*, of Chicago's Ninth Naval Training group steamed out into the lake. The crew standing at their posts observed the submarine only 20 to 30 miles east of Chicago. The sailors anxiously readied the weapons of the gunship.

The *S.S. Wilmette* was launched in 1903 at Port Huron, Michigan at the Jenks Shipbuilding Company for the Chicago Steamship Company. It was originally named the *S.S.*

UC-97 ---

*Eastland.* The ship was designed to transport passengers and cargo on Lake Michigan. Through its career it was known as a tender ship, meaning that it was prone to listing under light sea conditions regardless of its cargo.

On July 24, 1915 the *S.S. Eastland* earned the dubious distinction of being involved in the worst loss of life of any Great Lake shipping disaster.

On that summer day over 5,000 men, women and children crowded the docks along the Chicago River waiting to board one of the five passenger ships. The occasion was the Western Electric Annual Family Picnic.

The *Eastland* was the first to board and 2,570

*The German submarine UC-97. From the Leonard DeFrain Photographic Collection.*

people raced aboard and ran to the top deck to wave to their friends on shore. The ship listed to starboard; orders were given to trim the ship and take on ballast in the port tanks. The ship then listed to port, so orders were given to release port ballast and to take on starboard ballast. The ship listed to starboard again. They again took on port side ballast but the ship had listed so badly that river water began to pour into the ship through open gangways and portholes. Finally the ship rolled over on her port side sending hundreds into the river and trapping hundreds more below decks.

When the dead were counted, 814 men, women and children were killed on that day.

The *Eastland* was repaired and re-floated and put up for auction. The winning bid was from the Illinois Naval Reserve. They intended to use it for a training vessel. The United States Navy took over the vessel during World War I and moved it to the east coast but after the war she returned to the Great Lakes at her homeport of Chicago.

On June 7, 1921 the command to train the 4-inch guns of the *Wilmette* at the German submarine was given. When the order came to commence firing, the blasting of the guns shook the deck of the ship, deafening anyone close. The sailors of the *Wilmette* fired thirteen shells at the invading submarine; ten found their mark. The German submarine *UC-97* slowly sank to the bottom of Lake Michigan.

This is not fiction or the script of a movie. It's an actual account of the sinking of an authentic World War I German submarine in Lake Michigan just miles from Chicago.

But, let's back up a bit and relate… "The rest of the story." (Thank you Paul Harvey.)

Following the Armistice of November 11, 1918, which marked the end of hostilities of World War I, the United States was granted six captured German submarines: the *U-111*, *U-117*, *U-140*, *UB-88*, *UB-148* and the *UC-97*. The ships sailed from England to New York. From New York the submarines were assigned to various parts of the country to tour and

*The German submarine UC-97 on tour in the Great Lakes. Here the submarine and two escort vessels are docked allowing locals to tour the German submarine. From the collection of Leonard DeFrain.*

*The conning tower and some of the armament of the German Submarine* UC-97. *From the State of Michigan, Lansing, Michigan.*

promote a Victory Bond Drive. The *UC-97* was assigned to the Great Lakes region.

The German submarine *UC-97* embarked on a journey through the Canadian-controlled St. Lawrence Seaway. A German vessel passing through the seaway caused quite a stir among government officials. The submarine and her escort vessels, two naval sub-chasers *SC-411* and *SC-419*, eventually made it to the Great Lakes where they made a whirlwind tour of Lakes Ontario, Erie, Huron and Michigan.

The vessels stopped at ports large and small and allowed town folks to board and crawl all over the German vessel. The spectators then were given the Victory Bond pitch and bonds were sold in large numbers.

The *UC-97* developed engine troubles and it was necessary to cancel the Lake Superior leg of the tour, rather the submarine and its consorts went down Lake Michigan to Chicago. The *UC-97* was berthed at the Great Lakes Naval Station.

In 1921 the *UC-97* was showing signs of neglect and the cost to maintain the vessel had become a strain on the budget. According to the terms of the Armistice Treaty the submarine had to be destroyed. It was determined that the German submarine *UC-97* should be used for target practice. On June 7, 1921 the *UC-97* was towed some 20 miles east of Chicago and shelled by the *S.S. Wilmette* until she sank.

Many may think they have seen this submarine while visiting Chicago's Museum of Science and Industry, but that submarine on display is the *U-505*. The *U-505* is a German submarine from World War II while the *UC-97* was of World War I vintage.

In 1992, Taras Lyssenko and Al Olson located the wreck of the submarine *UC-97* on the bottom in over 300-feet of water. They say the submarine shows damage from only one shell striking her and they have determined that the vessel could be raised. Currently they are working through the maze of red tape and funding requirements in hopes to one day raise the only German submarine sunk on the Great lakes.

# THE HUNTER SAVIDGE VS. MOTHER NATURE

**S**trange weather phenomena is not uncommon on the Great Lakes. The Great Lake's basin size, almost 800 miles west to east and 500 miles north to south, and their geographical location create a variety of weather patterns. In 1899, the *Hunter Savidge* fell victim to one of Lake Huron's freaks of weather.

The *Hunter Savidge*, a 117-foot schooner, was built at Grand Haven, Michigan in 1879. She was a familiar sight in the ports of Lake Huron. It was said to be one of the best boats in her class, fast and very capable.

The ship had been owned by the firm of Savidge & Hunter of Ontario, but was sold to Mr. Phillip Mothorall of Alpena, Michigan. While owned by Mr. Mothorall, the *Hunter Savidge* collided with the schooner *Davis* off Bar Point in Lake Erie. The *Davis*, loaded with coal bound for Port Huron, sank in 21-feet of water. The *Hunter Savidge* received slight damage and was repaired during winter lay up.

Mr. John Muellerweiss, of Alpena, purchased the *Hunter Savidge* in 1892. Three years later she underwent a major overhaul, being almost entirely rebuilt. Mr. Muellerweiss held contracts to transport lumber south and coal north, contracts which proved very lucrative, and the *Hunter Savidge* was a perfect ship for the trade.

X-Hunter Savidge

*The* Hunter Savidge *under sail. From the Point Aux Barques Lighthouse Collection.*

In the 1899 season, Captain Fred Sharpsteen had been the Master of the *Hunter Savidge* for three seasons. He had a reputation among Great Lakes sailors as a careful and capable seaman.

On August 3, 1899, the schooner cleared Alpena downbound for Detroit with 10,000 cedar posts. On board were Captain Fred Sharpsteen, his wife Rose and 15-year old son John, the owner's wife, Mary Ann Muellerweiss, and their 5-year old daughter, Mate Thomas Dubuy, cook Charles Koch and sailor George Ellery. Mrs. Muellerweiss had never sailed on any of her husband's ships, but she had been ill and her doctor suggested that a trip might be beneficial to her. Mrs. Sharpsteen eagerly accompanied her on the voyage.

The trip down through Lake Huron was pleasurable and seemed to buoy the spirits of Mrs. Muellerweiss. It was early August, the days warm and the nights on the lake cool. The only problem encountered was an almost week long delay in unloading in Detroit. But the ladies took advantage of the layover and visited with friends and took in events the large city offered.

The *Hunter Savidge* left Detroit bound for Cleveland to take on a load of coal, then sailed back through the Detroit River into Lake St. Clair to the St. Clair River where the coal was discharged at Sarnia, Ontario.

The ladies enjoyed their stay in Sarnia, even hosting a party on board with friends from the area. Having no cargo consigned to take north, the *Hunter Savidge* took on two additional sailors wanting to go north. The schooner departed the river into Lake Huron on August 19, 1899.

The weather was calm with a light breeze. Captain Sharpsteen had all canvas out, and the ship sailing light made good way. That is until about 3:00 pm when the ship was about 8 miles off the Point aux Barques lighthouse. The winds ceased as a fog drifted in. The ship lay becalmed in a thick blanket of white.

Charles Koch was in the galley preparing the evening meal, while Mrs. Sharpsteen sat looking out a window wondering when they would reach Alpena. The Sharpsteen's were moving to Alpena on their return. They had met many new friends and she was anxious to set up housekeeping in a new house. Mrs. Muellerweiss reclined on a couch as Henrietta, affectionately called "Etta" by her adoring father, played on the floor of the cabin.

Captain Sharpsteen, Mate Dubuy, George Ellery, the two sailors who shipped on at Sarnia, Ed Bleel and Joslin Francis and the Captain's son

*The* Hunter Savidge *docked at Port Huron, Michigan. From the Point Aux Barques Lighthouse Collection.*

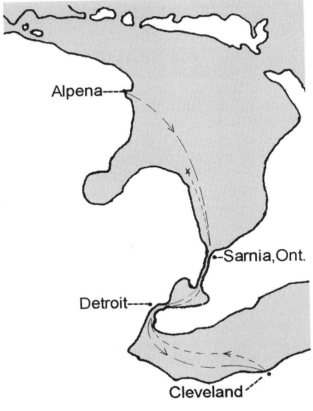

*The route of the* Hunter Savidge.

John were on the deck, keeping a look out for other ships and sounding the fog bell.

John had accompanied his father most of the season, and hoped to follow his father as a Great Lakes sailor; maybe some day he could be the master of his own ship.

On deck the thick fog coated every surface with moisture. The sails, all out in hope of catching a breeze, hung limp from the spars, dripping on the men below. Captain Sharpsteen asked his wife to get him his oilers to fend off the moisture.

Rose Sharpsteen looked around at the fog surrounding the ship as she handed the oilers to her husband. He remarked how it looked as if they were sailing in the clouds. Then she returned to the warmth and comfort of the cabin.

As Captain Sharpsteen began to slide his arm into his oilers, he stopped as he heard it approaching. Then, without time to react, a white squall bore down on the *Hunter Savidge*. The ship, lying becalmed with full sails, was not prepared for the whirlwind.

The wind quickly filled the sails, but without forward movement to compensate for the sideward force of the wind, the ship took a severe list to port. The ship would normally right herself as the gust ceased, but this was a steady blow of increasing velocity. The *Hunter Savidge* was blown over.

The ship hesitated, momentarily laying on her beam, then rolled over... bottom up. The ship once lay becalmed in a flat calm lake, now the lake assaulted the sinking vessel and the men hanging on to it with high winds and turbulent seas.

The sailors on deck were thrown into the lake. Captain Sharpsteen, still holding onto his oilers, clung to the ship. Two of the sailors surfaced close to him and the captain pulled them to the ship by heaving his oilers to them. The captain's

*Rose Sharpsteen. From the Point Aux Barques Lighthouse Collection.*

son John surfaced about 12-feet from his father clinging to some wood steps. His legs were caught in the rigging or his boots filled with water and he was drawn down again, not to reappear. John drowned before his father's eyes.

The cook, George Koch, trapped below in the galley, bleeding from a wound he sustained in the rollover, broke a window, crawled through and swam to the surface.

Mrs. Muellerweiss, Etta, and Mrs. Sharpsteen were trapped in the cabin. Captain Sharpsteen and the sailors heard their cries for help as the ship began to sink. There was nothing they could do, but listen to the women scream. Captain Sharpsteen had just watched his son drown, now there was nothing he could do for his wife. It was mental anguish no one should have to endure.

Just south of the *Hunter Savidge's* position was the upbound steamer *Alex McVitte*. The wheelman and captain of the *McVitte* could see the *Hunter Savidge* northeast of his position as he overtook the becalmed schooner. The captain observed the vessel as it was struck by the white squall and turned bottom up, in a matter of seconds. He changed course to go to the assistance of the capsized schooner.

Captain Sharpsteen and the sailors were taken on board the *McVitte*. Captain Sharpsteen and the captain of the *McVitte* surveyed the condition of the *Hunter Savidge*. Seeing no assistance could possibly be rendered to the *Hunter Savidge*, the ship continued north.

CHIGAN, MONDAY, AUGUST 21, 1899.

# AN APPALLING DISASTER.

### The Schooner Hunter Savidge Capsized off Point Aux Barques Sunday Evening.

## FIVE PEOPLE WERE DROWNED.

### Was Struck by a Squall About Two O'clock in the Afternoon.---Worst Marine Disaster of the Season.

Late Advices From Harbor Beach State That the Boat has Been Located, That the Bodies are in the Cabin and that the Wreck is Being Towed into Harbor.

ALL ARE RESIDENTS OF ALPENA EXCEPT ONE.

Mrs. Mary Ann Mullerweiss and Henrietta Mullerweiss, Wife and Daughter of the Owner; Mrs. Sharpsteen and Fred Sharpsteen, Wife and Son of the Captain, and Thomas Dubuy, Mate, are the Victims.

*Headline from the August 21, 1899, Alpena Evening News.*

Captain Sharpsteen wanted to go to the government harbor of refuge at Sand Beach since it was closest to the location of the sinking. When the *McVitte* met the southbound steamboat *H.G. Runnels*, the survivors were transferred to the *Runnels* to be taken to Sand Beach.

Once alerted of the accident, crews from the Sand Beach and Point aux Barques Life Saving station raced to the location of the wreck. They were joined by the tug *Angler* from the harbor with divers aboard and together they searched the area for signs of the wreck.

Captain Sharpsteen knew what he had to do next, the man who had lost his wife and son had to notify Mr. Mullerweiss of the loss of his wife, daughter and ship. A telegram was dispatched to Alpena. It read;

> *Harbor Beach*
> *August 20*
> *John Muellerweiss*             *Alpena, Michigan*
> Savidge *capsized 8 miles east of Point aux Barques in squall. Mrs. Muellerweiss and daughter, Captain's wife and son and mate drowned. Bring tug. Tug and divers go from here.*
> *F. Sharpsteen*

Upon receiving the telegram Mr. Muellerweiss was devastated. He surrounded himself with his two sons, Fred, age 17, Alfred, 13, and daughter Florence, 13, and friends. They relied on the strength of their church, friends and relatives to help them through the trying time.

The tug *Frank W.* was sent from Alpena to assist in the search efforts. Captain Lawson and Captain Lillies, both aboard, had orders from Mr. Muellerweiss to remain at the site of the accident until the *Hunter Savidge* was found… and bring the bodies of those who perished back to Alpena for a burial.

The *Frank W.* joined the search party on Monday morning. All upbound and downbound craft were notified to keep watch for the *Hunter Savidge*. It was emphasized that it may be floating almost totally submerged.

The Life Saving crews and tugs worked together in a systematic pattern looking for the vessel. They were later joined by a schooner that provided a perch in the rigging high above the lake's surface to better see at a distance. The search continued into Monday night and Tuesday morning until they were chased from the lake by weather. The tugs pulled the exhausted Life Savers and the schooner back to the harbor.

Late Monday Evening, Mr. Muellerweiss received the following telegram from Port Huron;

> *Port Huron, Michigan*
> *August 21*
> *John Muellerweiss*             *Alpena*
> Chemung *past here at 2 o'clock. Reported passing* Savidge *at 6 this morning, eight miles from Point aux Barques.*
> *Kindell Marine Reporting Co.*

*Captain Fred Sharpsteen after the sinking of the* Hunter Savidge. *From the Point Aux Barques Lighthouse Collection.*

This revelation gave new energy to the men searching the lake for the wreck of the *Hunter Savidge*. Unfortunately, Tuesday morning the seas were still too great for the ships to leave the harbor. The anxious men of the search vessels paced the wood deck of the breakwater pier staring out to the lake. They discussed the accident, their strategy, and the fate of those left in the cabin. The rescuers, after hearing the report from the propeller *Chemung*, reasoned that since the *Hunter Savidge* was sailing light, with no heavy cargo to quickly pull it to the bottom, the wood ship might yet be afloat. They were eager to get back out on the water to find the *Hunter Savidge*.

The news of the sighting filled the hearts of the Sharpsteen and Mullerweiss families with fresh hope that the bodies of those lost on the ship could be found alive or at least returned and buried for their eternal peace.

The *Chemung*, when arriving in Buffalo, received congratulations on finding the *Hunter Savidge*. The captain notified officials that it was incorrect. He had reported sighting the wreck of the schooner *Breeden*, which had foundered about five weeks earlier off Lexington.

On Wednesday August 23, 1899, three days since the freak storm Great Lake sailors call a "White Squall" over turned the *Hunter Savidge*, Captain Lillie of the tug *Frank W.* sent the following telegram to Mr. Mullerweiss:

*Harbor Beach*
*August 23*
*Mr. Mullerweiss*                                        *Alpena*
Chemung *report false. Have wired to that effect. Searched all morning with the boats and three tugs. Found nothing to give encouragement for further search.*
  *Thos. Lillie*

The search had been continued based on the strength of the report from the *Chemung*. Now since the report had been proven incorrect, the search was called off. The *Frank W.* and its saddened crew returned to Alpena. Those who had lost loved ones, their hopes of finding their bodies dashed, could now carry on with the mourning process.

A headline on the front page of the Saturday August 26 issue of the *Alpena Evening News* announced the *Hunter Savidge* was once again sighted. The tug *Frank W.* was being made ready to once again sail to the area. Another telegram from Harbor Beach was received by Mr. Mullerweiss:

*Harbor Beach*
*August 26*
*John Mullerweiss*                                        *Alpena*
*Tug* Carrie Martin *sighted* Savidge *eight miles southwest of here. Bow and stern out of the water. Tug brought in yawl which they cut loose from the wreck. No tug here large enough to tow her. No diver here.*
  *J. Jenks and Company*

Captain Edward Rice, Sand Beach Harbor Master, had accompanied the *Frank W.* on all searches and had not seen any indication that the *Hunter Savidge* was still afloat. Questioning the validity of the sighting, he investigated the claim that the yawl was from the *Savidge*. He found it was indeed from the *Savidge*. The fishermen said they even had to cut it loose from the davits.

He took a harbor tug to the location of the wreck. Despite another intensive search nothing was found but a tank from the missing ship.

Further discussions with the fishermen revealed what had occurred. They had indeed cut the yawl from the davits of the *Hunter Savidge*, but the davits had actually been ripped from the ship's deck. While the yawl was still tied to the davits, the davits were not attached to the ship.

Captain Rice telegrammed Mr. Mullerweiss to break the news to him that the *Hunter Savidge* had not been found.

The Keepers of the Point aux Barques and Sand Beach Life Saving Stations and Captain Rice surmised that since no valid sightings of the ship or wreckage had been found, the ship had most likely plunged to the bottom taking the men, women and child with it.

This news, the finality of it, was almost more than Mr. Mullerweiss could take. He sunk into a depression, which lasted several years. Captain

*The letter Captain Fred Sharpsteen wrote to his son. The letter is transcribed right. From the Point Aux Barques Lighthouse Collection.*

Sharpsteen, as well, had lost his wife and son, and he too was a lost sole longing for his loved ones. He was often seen walking the shore looking out into the lake, searching for his wife and son.

In the days that followed the last sighting, Alpena was a buzz with rumors and allegations. Why had Captain Sharpsteen left the ship while it was still afloat? Why didn't the captain of the *McVitte* take the *Savidge* in tow and pull it to shoal water? Why didn't he make an attempt to recover the bodies while the ship was still afloat? The citizenry cried out for the *McVitte* captain to be brought up on charges. Word was sent out on the lakes that should the captain ever visit Alpena he would be called on to explain such cowardly actions.

Both captains explained their decision to leave the *Hunter Savidge*. They said that the ship had turned bottom up so quickly that they felt nothing could be done. The ship was quickly filling and sinking as the survivors were taken aboard the *McVitte* and that no rescue of those trapped in the cabin could be made. The ship had sunk before them, they didn't leave it floating.

Captain Sharpsteen wrote his surviving son a letter on August 22, 1899, it read;

*"My dear son David, you are all I have in this world to help me mourn for our dear loved ones we have lost. I've bin trying to locate the reck, to get ma, but John drowned while hanging to some steps I think he was first. For if he could have swam ten feet I could have saved him. I saved cook and sailor with oil coat. I pulled them on to the reck. You get the* Detroit Free Press *and you will get the hole particulars which I rote last night. You tell Sluchler to deliver letter to Charley Hemerline or you take it up soon as you can. I have got to go to Alpena soon as I give up looking for schn. I lost every thing I've got a pair of pants and old shoes and sow western that is all I have to my name but what the folks give me. I will write more soon. I remain your Pa as ever.*

*F. Sharpsteen"*

# THE STRANGE AND TRAGIC TALE OF THE S.S. EASTLAND

On the morning of July 24, 1915 about 7,000 employees, families and guests of the Western Electric Company waited to board one of the five steamships moored along the Chicago River. The event was Western Electric's annual employee picnic. The ships would take the crowd to Michigan City, Indiana's Washington Park, where a full day of fun filled games and picnic meals waited.

The *S.S. Eastland*, a 265-foot long excursion ship was the first to board. The trip would depart at 7:30 am. Passengers began lining up long before that in hopes of being on the *Eastland*. It would be the first ship to depart, and it was the fastest of the five ships hired for the day.

Passengers poured through the gangways, and most ran up to the top decks where they could line the starboard rail to wave and yell to their friends still on the dock. The ship began to take on a slight list to starboard, which is normal when passengers gather dockside prior to departure.

An order was given from the bridge to the engine room to steady the ship. Valves were turned, and river water began to flow into the port ballast tanks. The ship righted as the water's weight countered the weight of the passengers at the starboard rail.

X---- S.S. Eastland

*The* S.S. Eastland. *From the photographic collection of the Port Huron Museum.*

Listing while loading was nothing unusual for a passenger ship. On a freighter, the cargo is carefully loaded and positioned to prevent the ship from becoming unstable. Yet on a passenger ship the human cargo does not evenly distribute their weight on the ship; in fact, the people are a mobile cargo which results in the ship constantly being trimmed. Typically as they board, large groups of passengers gather along one side and the ship needs to take on or pump out ballast to compensate.

The *Eastland* soon began to list to port, even though the largest congregation of passengers lined the starboard rail because there was too much ballast on the port side.

The Captain called the engine room with orders to take measures to compensate for the list. Below decks, ballast water is pumped from the port tanks and the ship slowly shifts back to an even keel.

2,500 passengers, the maximum amount the *Eastland* was certified to carry in 1913, had boarded the ship. Those waiting on the dock were diverted to the other four ships.

The *Eastland* began to again list to port.

# THE TALE OF THE S.S. EASTLAND

Captain Pedersen gave the order to prepare for immediate departure even though the ship remained unstable with a very noticeable list to port.

The *Eastland* continued with a list to port. Some passengers noticed the angle of the ship as they walked, but few were concerned. Yet, in the engine room, men frantically worked the valves to the ballast system, trying to trim the ship. As the stern line was released, the aft end of the ship drifted out into the river. The listing grew worse. Water began to pour in through the open port gangways and scuppers. The bilge pumps were started.

Captain Pedersen felt if he could get the ship out of the river into the open water of Lake Michigan, he could better deal with the problem. He called for a tug to escort the *Eastland* and asked for the drawbridge to be opened. The bridge master refused to open the bridge since he could see the ship was too unsteady to get underway.

The list to port of the ship dramatically increased as its stern floated free and the bow remained tied to the dock. Passengers began to scream as they could no longer ignore the list and began to slide across the decks

*The* S.S. Eastland *after capsizing in the Chicago River. From the Photographic Collection of the Port Huron Museum.*

**81**

towards the port side. Dishes could be heard breaking in the kitchen as they tumbled from the shelves.

Passengers in the main salon began to scream. The fun of the day turned to terror. Passengers ran as best they could to the deck in panic.

Tables and chairs slid to the port side, pinning people against the side wall. Water poured in port gangways while the boiler stokers, in a panic, climbed the ladder to escape a certain death as the water rose in the bilge. The pumps, already work-

*Passengers escape the* Eastland. *From the photographic collection of the Port Huron Museum.*

ing, struggled with the incoming water; it was coming in faster than they could pump it out.

On the main deck, passengers crawled on hands and knees attempting to save themselves. Others on the main deck jumped from the ship off the starboard side towards the dock. Some made the leap to the dock and some landed in the river.

As more water poured in through the gangways, the list worsened. Suddenly without hesitation, the list became too great for the ballast tanks to compensate, and the *Eastland* rolled onto her port coming to rest on the river bottom, her starboard hull exposed.

The ship, almost 40-feet in beam, settled to the bottom of the 20-foot deep river.

Those on the open decks were thrown or jumped from the ship into the river. The river's surface became alive with hundreds of bobbing heads screaming for help. Many, unable to swim or too scared, succumbed quickly to the river. Others looked to the thousands still lining the docks and screamed for help.

Passengers aboard the other ships still tied to the docks looked on in horror as their friends, just moments before happy and gay with the anticipation of the day's events, died before their eyes. A lifeboat and life rafts from the *Eastland* floated free but floated empty in the sea of drowning passengers and crew.

Life preservers, deck chairs, and anything that would float was thrown to the screaming throngs in the water. Lifeboats were hurriedly lowered from nearby ships. Many victims were taken aboard, but the immensity of the disaster was so great that many of the passengers cast into the river were overcome by panic and shock and died in the water.

Those on the open decks who were cast into the river were the lucky ones. Many passengers were trapped below decks. Those in cabins on the port side were drowned as the ship rolled over and filled with river water. The unfortunate souls who were along the port cabin walls were crushed by the weight of others thrown against them as the ship overturned. Cries came from the mass of humanity stacked several deep. Some tried to claw out of the mass of carnage. The water crept up, slowly drowning those not

*The* Eastland *being readied for righting. From the photographic collection of the Port Huron Museum.*

# STRANGE & UNUSUAL SHIPWRECKS ON THE GREAT LAKES

*The* Eastland *lies on the bottom of the Chicago River. From the photographic collection of the Port Huron Museum.*

killed by the weight of the others. Soon the screams and cries for help subsided as the passengers drowned within the confines of the ship.

Many were trapped in cabins, passageways, or other areas with no means of escape, screaming for help as the water slowly rose. They drew in a deep breath as the water neared their heads, only to involuntarily exhale and suck in river water, filling their lungs to die an agonizing death.

Families huddled together, nowhere to go, as water crept up around them. Fathers and mothers held their children high as the water rose to no avail. The families died together. Many children, mothers and fathers were later found locked in a deadly embrace. Twenty-two entire families were killed on the fateful morning.

Some, trapped below decks, had to step on the bodies of their dead friends as they tried to find a way to escape death. Portholes on the starboard side were opened, and those small enough to fit through climbed out to join the several hundred passengers and crew who had made it to safety.

Some passengers lucky enough to be close to a starboard gangway were able to climb or be pulled to the side of the vessel lying above the river's surface. Rescuers reached down into the gangways to the mass of people climbing on one another, trying to escape the ship. Many were pulled to safety while others were crushed by the panicked. Hundreds stood on the starboard side of the ship, shaken, many in shock but alive.

The Chicago Police and Fire Departments were quick to respond to the capsizing. Tugs and other boats nearby steamed to the area. Dead bodies were pushed aside to gain access to those still alive, floundering in the river. Several people from the crowd on the wharf dove into the river to rescue those in the screaming mass. Some victims reached out for anything that could save them, life preservers and furniture thrown from the other ships and wood ripped from the wharf. Some of the panicked grabbed other passengers and drowned them in an attempt to save themselves.

The Tug *Kenosha* was now pulling passengers from the river. "Save those who can be saved!"cried the captain, as dead were ignored and only those showing movement were pulled to safety. Some men openly cried as they used pike poles to push away floating bodies to reach those showing life.

Pounding from inside the hull could be heard by rescuers and survivors standing on the starboard hull. The trapped pounded and scratched at the hull, hoping someone would hear their signal and rescue them. Firemen on the starboard side of the ship used their axes on the wood cabin structure to release passengers trapped inside. Soon men arrived with cutting torches. The torches cut large holes in the starboard hull, allowing many to escape. Rescue workers jumped in through the holes and pulled the injured to safety. Later, as the water increased, the rescue workers in the hull waded in the water, feeling with their feet for the bodies of the dead.

The dead, by the hundreds, were brought out of the ship and river during the day and into the night. The screams of joy as the passengers boarded, were replaced with cries for help, then tears for the dead. On that fateful morning of July 24, 1915, 815 people died as the *Eastland* rolled over to port.

The capsizing of the *S.S. Eastland* was the deadliest disaster to ever occur on the Great Lakes. Strangely, ironically, and tragically the ship was still tied to the dock!

*Authors note:* Special thanks to the *Eastland* Disaster Historical Society, PO Box 2013, Arlington Heights, IL 60006-2013, 1-877-865-6295, www.eastlanddisaster.org.

# THE WINDOC
# AND THE BRIDGE

**T**he Welland Canal is an approximately 27-mile waterway which allows maritime traffic to travel between Lake Erie and Lake Ontario. The canal has eight locks to raise or lower the ships from the level of Lake Erie down to the level of Lake Ontario. Also crossing the Welland Canal are more than 20 bridges.

Anytime there are that many bridges on a busy waterway like the Welland Canal, there are bound to be ship and bridge accidents. One of the most unusual is the August 11, 2001 incident involving the 730-foot *Windoc*.

The *Windoc*, owned by N.M. Paterson and Sons Ltd., was in normal transit up the canal after having taken on a cargo of 26,000 metric tons of grain in Thunder Bay, Ontario bound for Montreal.

Having traveled about 12 miles up the canal, Captain Ken Strong, wheelsman, and the ship's third officer were in the pilothouse as they approached the Allanburg Bridge, bridge #11.

The Allanburg Bridge is a vertical lift bridge. The entire span raises to permit maritime traffic to pass below unobstructed. The bridge operators control room is mounted above the roadbed and raises with the span.

Windoc---X

*The* Windoc. *From the collection of Jeff Cameron.*

As the *Windoc* approached bridge 11, the men in the pilothouse observed the flashing amber approach light. A series of colored lights had been developed to allow communication between the bridge operator and the vessels passing through it. The amber light indicated that the bridge operator was aware that the vessel was approaching.

As the *Windoc* drew closer to the span, a flashing red light was seen as the span was being raised. When the roadbed was raised to its full extent the light changed to solid green. The *Windoc* lined up with the center line of the bridge and proceeded under it.

When the *Windoc* was about halfway through the bridge, the third officer noticed that the bridge span was descending!

Captain Strong quickly sounded several blasts on the ship's whistle and called on the VHF radio to the Traffic Control Center to inform them that the bridge was lowering prematurely.

The *Windoc*, built in 1959, was designed with the superstructure and wheelhouse at the stern, rather than at the bow as earlier Great Lakes freighters. The superstructure had not yet cleared the bridge span!

The radio call and the blasting of the ship's whistle had no effect on the bridge, it continued to lower. The ship was unable to stop in time to avoid a collision with the vertical lift bridge's roadbed.

# THE WINDOC AND THE BRIDGE

Captain Strong ordered everyone out of the wheelhouse, a collision was imminent. All left but the wheelsman, Alan Hiscock. Mr. Hiscock was fearful that the ship would drift out of control if he left the wheel, so he laid on the deck as the ship struck the bridge.

The *Windoc* rammed the Allanburg Bridge at about the level of the wheelhouse. The windows smashed inward, the steel of the superstructure ripped with a metallic shriek. Much of the wheelhouse was pushed backward onto the crew quarters. With the ship still powering forward, the exhaust stack (smokestack) was next to be struck by the bridge. The structural steel and concrete of the bridge gave way in a crunching sound until the stack was ripped from the deck. The stack toppled backwards landing on the aft deck.

The starboard anchor of the *Windoc* was released in an attempt to stop the crippled ship. The ship swung around until it came to rest about a half of a mile beyond the bridge, the bow against the east bank and the *Windoc's* stern was embedded in the west bank, effectively blocking the waterway.

Smoke was detected coming from the crew quarters, and soon flames were climbing into the sky from the stricken ship. The crew had mustered at the sound of the signal whistle and were now breaking out the

*The damage to the bridge is visible at the center of the photograph. From the collection of David J. Wobser.*

**89**

*The damaged* Windoc *the day after the accident. From the collection of David J. Wobser.*

*The damage to the stern section of the* Windoc. *From the collection of David J. Wobser.*

*The* Windoc *the day after the accident rests on the bottom after the fire was extinguished. From the collection of David J. Wobser.*

firefighting equipment. Area firefighters responded quickly to fight the rapidly spreading fire. Streams of water were pumped onto the burning aft section of the *Windoc* from both sides of the canal.

The fire took a day to extinguish. In the end, the accident resulted in no deaths, but the fate of the *Windoc* was a big question. It might be too expensive to repair. The Allanburg Bridge was damaged and could not be used, it was stuck partially in the up position. Vessel traffic on the Welland Canal was halted. Many ships anchored or docked where ever they could to await passage through the seaway.

After days of inspection by engineers, the bridge was raised to the up position. The *Windoc* was towed so it was no longer blocking the canal and vessel traffic once again could traverse the canal.

The bridge operator claimed that he could see the stern of the *Windoc* passing and that he thought the ship had passed the tower. However, his judgment may have been impaired by the fact that he finished working his regular shift on that day and was working overtime, or maybe the prescription pain killer he had taken impaired his judgment, or maybe it was the two to four glasses of wine he admitted to drinking at lunch.

# THE CHARLES H. BRADLEY LOSES IN THE END

**T**here is an old adage; "Sometimes you win, sometimes you lose."

Or in the Great Lakes region there is another way of stating the same thing: "Sometimes you eat the bear, and sometimes the bear eats you." Such is the case of steamer *Charles Bradley*.

The *Charles Bradley* was a 201-foot wood vessel built in 1890. Originally she was engaged in transporting lumber from the upper lakes to the growing populations establishing themselves along the lower Great Lakes. On July 18, 1920 the *Bradley* had been contracted by O.W. Blodgett Company of Duluth, Minnesota to tow its barges, the *Mystic* and the *Blodgett*, loaded with salt from Buffalo, New York to Duluth.

The barges would be towed across the length of Lake Erie, through the Detroit River, into Lake St. Clair and the St. Clair River. From there the vessels would enter Lake Huron, travel her length into the St. Marys River and through the locks at Sault Ste. Marie. Then the long sail the length of Lake Superior was all that remained, a course that would cover almost 1,000 miles.

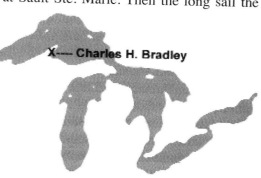

X—— Charles H. Bradley

About halfway into the trip on Lake Huron off Thunder Bay, a summer storm, with wind whipped seas was encountered.

The *Charles Bradley*,

the barges at the end of the tow line, rounded Sturgeon Point about 26 miles south of Alpena, Michigan.

Captain Jordan, Master of the steamer, found conditions to worsen. The wind and the seas were such that his ship, towing the barges, could not maintain headway.

Captain Jordan made the decision not to proceed but to lay to into the wind and await more favorable conditions. The steamer lowered her anchor to ride out the storm.

The tremendous combination of high seas and gale force winds rendered the three ships helpless. Trying to maintain a position with the seas pounding on them was a task. The barges pitched and rolled violently at the end of their tether. The crew on board the barges feared for their safety, knowing that at anytime the manila towline, their lifeline to the steamer, could part and leave them to helplessly adrift about in the violent seas, death an almost certainty.

Onboard the *Charles Bradley*, Captain Jordan stared out the windows of the pilothouse. He silently questioned himself; "Will the anchors hold? Should he have tried to make the safety of Thunder Bay? When will these hellish conditions cease?"

For over four hours the three vessels were assaulted by all that Lake Huron could throw at them. The lake's storms are legendary and strike fear in even the most seasoned sailor.

The *Bradley* held her bow into the wind, and was riding out the storm. The barges behind her were thrashing about wildly in the storm.

The barges, secured at the bow with the tow line, were restricted in their ability to ride the waves. The barges might rise up on the crest of a wave but with the towline taut the vessels couldn't crest with the waves, rather the bow would be pulled down into the wave. Tons of water would smash down on the ship. Torrents of water cascaded aft washing away anything not secured.

Aboard the *Bradley*, Captain Jordan worried about the barges. They were taking a beating. He worried that they might swing on the towline and ram the *Bradley*. His fears were soon realized as the barge *Blodgett* surged forward on a particularly large wave and smashed into the stern of the *Bradley*.

Wood splintered in a horrible crashing crescendo. The bow of the barge was smashed in and thousands of gallons of angry Lake Huron water poured into the gash.

# THE CHARLES H. BRADLEY LOSES IN THE END

The stern of the *Bradley* was smashed in by the impact with the barge. She started taking on water as well. Orders on both vessels were given to the crew to man the pumps before the level reached a critical point.

Captain Jordan ordered rockets to be sent aloft. He also sent out an urgent S.O.S. call on the wireless radio.

The Wyandotte Transportation Company's steamer, the *Huron*, received the S.O.S. and, in the tradition of the Great Lakes, changed its course to speed to the stricken vessels.

In Alpena the tug *Owen* heard the *Bradley's* S.O.S. and set out from the shelter of the bay to take the barges in tow and bring them to safety. No sooner had the tug arrived on site than one of the barges sank below the surface. The crew had been taken off by the *Huron*.

It was decided that the *Charles Bradley* had to get into the harbor. Her pumps weren't keeping up with the water coming in through her damaged stern. The *Huron* would tow her and the *Owen* would steer her from the stern. As they were setting up, the *Owen* sprung a leak and had to depart and race for shore. The captain was about to call for the crew to abandon the sinking tug when the leak miraculously stopped. The tug made it to safety and was repaired by the next day.

The *Huron* towed the *Bradley* in and the barge *Miztec* was brought in by another vessel. The sunken barge could not be raised, and the *Bradley* was repaired to continue sailing.

The *Charles Bradley* was involved in another incident eleven years later. This time it occurred in Michigan's Upper Peninsula.

The Portage Ship Canal, built in the 1860's and today known as the Keweenaw Waterway, was originally called the Portage Lake and Lake Superior Ship Canal. It was intended to connect Keweenaw Bay (on the East) through Portage Lake into Lake Superior (on the West). The canal was designed to save at least 100 miles, valuable time and money for a vessel traveling around the Kewaunee Peninsula.

On October 9, 1931 the steamer *Charles Bradley* carried a deck load of pulpwood bound for Georgian Bay. She was also towing the 218-foot barge *Grampian* which was traveling light.

The two vessels entered the Ship Canal from the west side of the Keweenaw Peninsula and had passed through the canal and Portage Lake and were preparing to enter the east entry to the Portage River.

Captain Golomblaky, master of the *Bradley*, stood at the bridge of his ship watching for the light which marked the entrance. He looked but could not find the light; the navigational beacon had failed.

Without the light to guide the steamer, the *Bradley* veered too far off the channel and drove up hard on a sand bar.

The *Charles Bradley* stopped dead in the water. Unfortunately the *Bradley's* barge, the *Grampian*, didn't have brakes. Unable to stop its momentum, the *Grampian* towed behind the *Bradley* smashed into the stern of the stranded steamer.

The *Grampian* wasn't too badly damaged, but in the crash, electrical conduit and steam pipes were broken. Near the deckhouse a fire started between the walls.

Since the steam line was broken, the fire pumps wouldn't operate. The crew fought the fire with buckets and hand pump extinguishers.

The flames, fed on the dry pulpwood cargo, were out of control. It soon seemed to the captain that the *Bradley* was doomed and he gave the abandon ship order.

The men took to the lifeboats and a yawl from the *Grampian*. The men pulled on the oars to get away from the inferno of the *Bradley*, then turned to watch the 41-year-old steamer burn to the waterline.

The *Grampian* was not badly damaged in the collision but the *Bradley* was destroyed.

In the 1920 incident, the *Charles Bradley's* barge *Mary Woolson* crashed into the stern of the steamer and the barge sank. In the 1931 collision, the barge *Grampian* smashed into the stern of the *Bradley* and the *Bradley* was destroyed.

# THE FIFTH TRIP OF THE WILLIAM C. MORELAND

**O**n July 27, 1910 the big steamer *William C. Moreland* slid down the ways of the American Shipbuilding Company to start her career of carrying iron ore from the mines of the upper Midwest to the steel furnaces of the lower lakes.

The brand new ship was fitted out and her first trip was in September of 1910. Her owners were anxious to recoup the cost of building the ship, $450,000.00, and start making a profit.

The *Moreland* measured 580-feet in length with a gross tonnage of 8,800. The new ship fell into the routine of loading iron ore from Duluth and Marquette to the steel mills along Lake Erie. The new ship was a favorite to see passing through the locks and the St. Clair and Detroit Rivers.

On the fifth trip of its existence, the large ship had taken on a cargo at Superior, Wisconsin and cleared the dock early in the morning of October 18, 1910.

Captain Ennes set a northeast course for the ship that would take her out from the harbor and across the top of the Keweenaw Peninsula. Once rounding the peninsula, a course change to southeast would be made

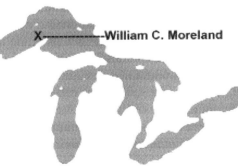

*The* William C. Moreland *grounded and ice covered. From the State of Michigan Archives, Lansing, Michigan.*

taking the vessel to the locks at the Soo, then down Lake Huron arriving in Lake Erie to off load the ore. It was nothing out of the ordinary, just another routine trip.

The ship's passage should take it about 1-1/2 - 2 miles off the rocky coast of the Keweenaw. That course would provide more than enough water under her keel.

On that day in mid October, there was another event occurring that would impact the big *William C. Moreland*, this one on land.

In the early 1900's the vast forests of the upper Midwest supplied millions of board feet of lumber to meet the needs of the growing populations of the urban areas. The method that was employed by the lumber men was to cut down a tree, de-limb it and cut the trunk into manageable lengths.

The limbs and branches were left on the forest floor to decay. Unfortunately, the branches dried and all too often were prone to catch fire.

Forest fires were a constant hazard for the men working the woods. But the fires were also a source of concern for the ships on the lakes.

The burning trees produced huge amounts of smoke. The smoke often hung low over the water, hampering visibility. Many maritime accidents were caused by the smoke produced by forest fires.

The smoke from the onshore blaze laid low on the water. Captain Ennes looked out the wheelhouse windows, wishing he could see land to verify his position, but the smoke obstructed his view of shore.

# THE FIFTH TRIP OF THE WILLIAM C. MORELAND

Two hundred miles into the trip, at about 9:00 pm, the 580-foot ship traveling at full speed, suddenly ground to a stop. The *William Moreland* was not the 1-1/2 to 2 miles off the peninsula as they thought. Rather they were less than a mile and the ship had run up on Sawtooth Reef off Eagle Harbor, Michigan.

The notorious Sawtooth Reef has seen the demise of many ships. The 254-foot steamer *Colorado* in 1898 and the 65-foot tug, *Fern* were lost on the reef in 1901 while trying to salvage the *Colorado*. The *Moreland* would not be the last to meet the reef either. In 1919 the 258-foot iron packet freighter *Tioga* was destroyed by the reef.

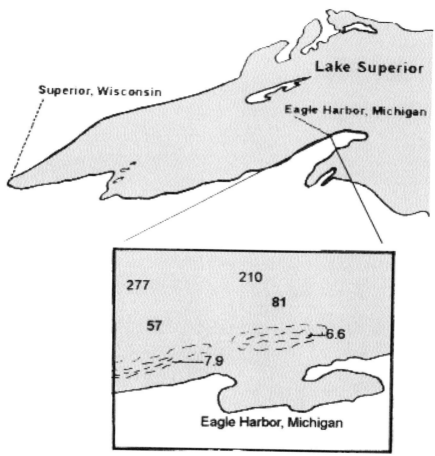

*The* William C. Moreland *struck Sawtooth Reef off Eagle Harbor, Michigan. The numbers in the lower drawing indicate depths in feet.*

Captain Ennes ordered the telegraph to full astern in an attempt to back the ship off the reef. The three-month-old ship wasn't budging; it had run hard aground on the jagged rocky reef just a few feet below the surface.

The *Moreland* had sustained damage to her hull and began taking on water. The crew fought to slow the incoming torrents of water, but by morning a storm started blowing and Captain Ennes ordered the men to the waiting boats of the Portage Ship Canal Lifesaving station. The ship wasn't in jeopardy of sinking, she was hard aground.

Once the storm had blown out, the captain and crew were able to return to their ship. They raised steam in her boilers but before an attempt at powering off the reef could be made, the large steel ship developed a crack between hatches 10 and 11. The brand new ship, supported on the reef at her bow, with an un-supported aft, began to break in two.

Tom Reid, owner of Reid Wrecking and Towing Company, was awarded the bid to salvage the *William C. Moreland*. He and a crew set out from their quarters at Sarnia, Canada aboard the wrecking tugs *Manistique* and *Sarnia*.

Under the direction of the captain, almost 7,000 tons of iron ore were removed from the *Moreland* in hopes that the lighter craft might be able to be repaired and floated free of the reef. Unfortunately the big vessel was held fast to the rocky bottom.

*The stern section of the* William C. Moreland *being towed by a* Reid *tug.*
*From the State of Michigan Archives, Lansing, Michigan.*

*The only time "half" of a boat locked through at the Soo. From the State of Michigan Archives, Lansing, Michigan.*

Captain Reid continued to remove the cargo but they were often chased from the lake by the tremendous fall storms that lash out at Lake Superior. In a violent storm, the *Moreland* cracked between hatches 22 and 23. The once new 580-foot long ship was now divided into three pieces! Due to the storms and the onset of heavy ice, the salvaging of the wreck of the *William C. Moreland* had to be put off until spring.

When the weather cleared, the open ends of the broken vessel were closed in with temporary bulkheads and pumped out. Then in July of 1911 the three sections were lashed together and floated free of the reef.

While being towed, the *Moreland*, incapable of steering, collided with the tug *James Reid*. The temporary patches began to leak and the ship took on more water than the pumps could handle. The *William C. Moreland* once again sank on Sawtooth Reef. This time the vessel was on a deeper part of the reef and only part of her superstructure remained visible.

Another severe Lake Superior storm pounded down on the crippled vessel separating the 278-foot stern section from the other two sections. Efforts were turned to salvaging the valuable stern section with its new triple expansion steam engines. They could be recovered and sold for use in another ship.

The stern section was temporarily repaired, raised by mid August and the Reid Wrecking and Towing Company towed the stern of the once brand new *William C. Moreland* almost 550 miles to Detroit.

The bow sections of the *Moreland* in time were assaulted by other storms and eventually slid off the reef into deeper water. The stern section was moved again to Port Huron where she was beached, waiting for someone to place a bid on her scrap value.

The *William C. Moreland*, 580-feet in length 58-feet wide and only months old when she ran up hard on Sawtooth Reef now almost two years earlier, was not going to go easily to the scrap yard. Fortunately, the Canadian Steamship Lines saw some usefulness left in the wreck and purchased it.

Construction began on a new 322-foot bow section in Superior, Wisconsin. The Reid Wrecking and Towing Company again took the remains of the *William C. Moreland* stern back up to Lake Superior to mate with her new forward section.

The new, actually half new, ship was christened in November of 1916 the Sir Trevor Dawson. The vessel sailed on the lakes until World War One when she was laid up. In 1920 the Dawson was sold and became the *Charles L. Hutchinson*.

She continued to be a profitable carrier and in 1951 her name was again changed, this time to *Gene C. Hutchings*. In 1962 another sale brought about another name change to *Parkdale*.

The once mighty *William C. Moreland* was retired in 1968. Throughout those years the vessel saw a lot of service on the lakes and tragedy as well. In June of 1970 the ship sailed her last voyage. The last trip was to Cartagena, Spain for an appointment at the scrap yard. But the ship had beaten the odds and survived to a ripe old age of fifty eight... well half of her anyway.

# LOADING OF THE ANN ARBOR #4

**T**he history of the Ann Arbor Railroad and of the railroad's car ferries would take volumes to contain. This section will include only the mishaps of one of the car ferries, the *Ann Arbor #4*.

The railroad began operations in 1878 to provide service between Toledo, Ohio and Frankfort, Michigan. The cargo traveled by rail to Frankfort where it was off loaded onto ships and taken across Lake Michigan. At a Wisconsin port, the ship was off-loaded and the cargo was again put on rail cars to continue to its destination.

This was a time consuming and expensive way to transport the cargo. In September of 1892 the Ann Arbor Railroad launched its first car ferry, the 260-foot *Ann Arbor #1*. The advancement allowed the rail cars to be loaded directly onto the ferry, no longer requiring the off-loading and reloading of cargo. The wood hulled vessel could carry 24 fully loaded rail cars. The cars were rolled onto rails on the ship and chained in place.

When the ferry reached the other side of the lake, the cars were rolled off and coupled to a waiting locomotive.

After some initial hesitation from those shipping the cargo, the *Ann Arbor #1* was a huge financial success. The railroad

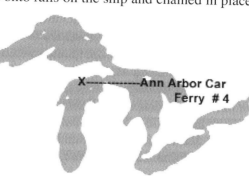

X----------Ann Arbor Car
Ferry # 4

*The car ferry* Ann Arbor #4. *From the State of Michigan Archives, Lansing, Michigan.*

eventually built eight ferries between 1892 and 1925 which served several ports along the Wisconsin and Michigan coasts of Lake Michigan.

The *Ann Arbor #2* was similar to the *#1*, with a wood hull and about the same length and capacity. The *Ann Arbor #3* was the first of the ferries to be constructed with a steel hull. This enabled the vessel to operate longer into the winter with ice breaking ability. The *Ann Arbor #3* made runs across the lake and also transported freight and rail cars from Manistique in Michigan's Upper Peninsula to its home port of Frankfort.

The *Ann Arbor #4* was launched in 1906 with a length of 258-feet. The vessel was built with four tracks and a capacity of 24 rail cars. The *Ann Arbor #4's* career could best be described as fraught with mishap.

Three years after her launch, the ferry was rounding a point at the top of Lake Michigan in preparation to enter Manistique Harbor when she went aground. Try as they might, her two triple expansion engines couldn't back her off.

Two men went ashore in a yawl to call for assistance. The two men endured the cold January 24th winds and pulled to shore through a frigid Lake Michigan. They secured their boat and set out on an eight mile walk, in snow drifts, to Thompson, Michigan. There they were able to call for a harbor tug in Manistique to pull the big ferry off the rocky shoal.

The men started back en route to the stranded ferry, walking the eight miles back to the yawl and rowing back to the *Ann Arbor #4*. As they approached they were surprised to see the boat was no where to be found. It was gone!

In their absence, the wind had shifted and the ferry was able to work off the shoal under her own power. The men were tired and found an old wrecked schooner that had been washed ashore years earlier and settled in for the night. The next day they met up with the *Ann Arbor #4* in Manistique.

Manistique was again the location of another *Ann Arbor #4* incident. On May 29, 1909, the ferry was moored to the loading dock preparing to take on a cargo of 24 hopper cars of iron ore, 1,200 tons in all.

"Human error"is a nice catch phrase that is used to describe an accident where we humans screw up. Human error was the cause of the *Ann Arbor #4's* problems on that May 1909 day.

The *Ann Arbor #4* was equipped with four rails running the length of the vessel. The center two rails could carry eight fully loaded railcars each. The outer, or starboard and port wing rails, each could hold four railcars each. Once on board the railcars were chained and dogged down so they couldn't shift and make the vessel unstable. But the loading and off-loading procedure of the railcars was the most critical part of the operation.

In Manistique, the railroad engineer switched the hopper cars filled with the heavy iron ore until he had four hoppers coupled to five empty flat cars, called idler cars. The purpose of the idler cars is to reduce the total weight on the ship at any one time and to keep the switch locomotive off the vessel and the apron. (The approach to the vessel.)

The four hopper cars were pushed aboard the center set of starboard tracks, with the five idler cars between the loaded cars and the locomotive. The ore cars were uncoupled and the idler cars backed off. The idler cars were then coupled to eight loaded hopper cars, with idler cars between the load and the locomotive. They were pushed onto the center port tracks. The remaining four ore cars were then pushed onto the center starboard track. There were 16 fully loaded ore cars placed on the vessel according to company procedure.

The next step in the loading of the car ferry was to load two ore cars on the port wing, four on the starboard wing and then the final two on the port side. This would keep the *Ann Arbor #4* on an even trim throughout the loading.

*Hopper cars being removed from the* Pere Marquette #4. *From the Port Huron Museum.*

The railroad engineer operating the switch engine coupled to a cut of eight loaded ore cars. Rather than use idler cars to push the two cars onto the port wing tracks, he pushed all eight onboard the ship. His intention was that the two front cars would be uncoupled, he would back off the remaining six cars, place four on the starboard wing track and then place the last two ore cars on the port wing track.

It didn't work quite like he planned. The *Ann Arbor #4* began to list to port under the weight of the eight heavy iron ore filled railcars. The engineer saw the list and began to back off the ferry, but the list caused a coupling between the hopper cars to break, leaving the heavy load on the port side of the ship.

The crew looked on in horror as the *Ann Arbor #4* slowly rolled to port. Nothing could be done. As the list increased, water poured into the ferry through open deadlights (portholes). As the list increased from the weight of the water pouring in, the railcars began to topple over to port, spilling the cargo of ore, crushing interior stanchions and destroying the ships stack. The weight of the hopper cars caused the *Ann Arbor #4* to roll until she settled on the bottom, resting on her port side.

It was a slow roll. From the time of the first list until the ferry settled to the bottom was about ten minutes. All crew had time to get off the ship safely. Some even had time to retrieve personal belongings.

*The destruction to the hopper cars and the interior of the* Ann Arbor #4. *From the State of Michigan Archive, Lansing, Michigan.*

A departure from standard practice had caused the capsizing of the *Ann Arbor #4*. A short cut which might have worked with lighter cargo resulted in a very expensive salvage operation. While the ship laid in the river for over a month, the wreckers had to remove several of the hull plates on her starboard to lift out the wrecked and twisted railcars from the *Ann Arbor #4*. The ship then underwent an extensive and expensive re-fitting.

The *Ann Arbor #4* continued to serve on the Great Lakes for another 65 years. In 1937 she was sold to the State of Michigan for use as an automobile ferry across the Straights of Mackinaw under the name City of Cheboygan. She served in that capacity until 1960 when the vessel was again sold and turned into a floating warehouse, storing potatoes. In 1974 the *Ann Arbor #4* was scrapped in Italy.

The vessel experienced a career of almost 68 years, but not without several mishaps, but it was human error that did her in at Manistique, Michigan.

# KEEPER CAPTAIN KIAH AND HIS HEROIC SURFMEN

**T**he horrendous events, which surround the heroic and tragic attempted rescue by the Port Aux Barques Life Saving Station, have often been told. Yet it is an historical event that exemplifies the dedication and strength of the men of the Life Saving Service.

April in Michigan's Thumb area is beautiful. The cold of winter gives way to the sun and milder temperatures of spring. The trees bud and the fields start to turn green with growth, the lake is an inviting sight as well.

But, Lake Huron does not give up winter's cold easily. The lake doesn't reach swimming temperature until late June, although some say it never does. Working on the lakes is wrought with inherent dangers. The spring, with its storms, cold winds, and near freezing water temperatures multiply the potential troubles. The worst of the dangers is the cold lake water. The cold of the water will quickly rob a person of strength and reasoning. The life expectancy for a person in the icy water is short, very short.

Captain Jerome Kiah and his crew were called out on April 23, 1880. The scow *Magruder* loaded with 187,000-feet of lumber was down bound from Alcona for Detroit when a spring storm struck the lake. The

X----Captain Kiah

ship was off the Point aux Barques lighthouse when its hull began to leak and was listing badly to port. Men were put to the pumps, but despite the constant pumping, 11-feet of water had filled her hull.

Captain J. H. Cronkey, both owner and Captain of the *Magruder*, knew he could not sail to the harbor at Sand Beach with a heavy non responsive ship, it would certainly roll in the seas. He elected to run for the shallows off Huron City.

In 14-feet of water he ordered both anchors released, but with each surge of the waves the anchors would drag along the bottom. The *Magruder* may have been in shallow water but not out of danger. She was laying bow to the east and taking the waves over the bow. The ship, laying more than two miles from shore, was in peril. The crew needed to get off the ship before it was smashed on the rocks.

On board the schooner *Magruder* were the Captain, four crewmen, the Captain's wife and their two small children. They raised a red lantern in the rigging, and lowered their flag to half-mast, signs of distress. Then they prayed someone would find them before the ship broke up on the reef and they were thrown into the cold waters of Lake Huron.

Captain Jerome Kiah, the keeper of the Life Saving Station at Point aux Barques, saw the signal and ordered a surfman to light a Coston flare to answer the ship that their distress signal had been seen.

By 7:30 that morning the crew had made ready to go to the ship. Captain Kiah knew the waves breaking on the reef and rocks in the notoriously shallow area posed a challenge to the crew. He elected to use the station surfboat rather than the lifeboat for it was better in the breakers.

Onboard the boat was Captain Kiah, Robert Morrison of Caseville, William Sayres of Port Austin, James Pottinger from Huron City, Dennis Degan of Grindstone City and Walter Petherbridge and Jas. Nantan, both from Walkerville.

The surfboat slid down the rails from the boathouse, splashing into the icy Lake Huron water and they set out into the angry sea and east wind towards the *Magruder* about three miles southeast of the station.

Captain Kiah at the stern with the steering oar, and six surfmen manning the oars, fought to keep the surfboat into the waves while maneuvering around rocks and avoiding the shallow reefs. After almost two hours they had rowed beyond the breakers on the reef and were now in the deeper water. But they were not out of danger.

Captain Cronkey, master of the *Magruder*, watched the surfboat as it was struck by a tremendous sea and was tossed into the air, men and oars flying about. The surfmen were prepared for such an event, righting and bailing the surfboat, was something they had relentlessly practiced. Captain Kiah was a task master when it came to drilling on the righting of the surfboat. It's a skill, he told the men, which someday might save your life.

The crew, floating in their cork jackets, quickly gathered their oars before they were washed away. As in the drill, they all gathered on the lee side of the upturned boat, hanging onto the boat's lifelines. They climbed on the gunnels, their weight forcing the boat to turn over. Once righted, the surfmen would carefully crawl on so not to upset the boat again, and begin to bail it out.

The men, sitting in cold April Lake Huron water, resumed their efforts towards the *Magruder*. They could see the ship's crew on the deck watching with anticipation of their rescue. The looks of fear on their faces spurred on the Life Saving crew. Captain Kiah was shouting words of encouragement to his boys when another wave over took the surfboat and again it capsized.

The weary crew worked to right the boat, but this time they were just too exhausted. Every movement took effort the men no longer could muster. Captain Kiah ordered the men to just hang onto the lifelines to regain strength before their next attempt to right her.

Captain Cronkey, only a quarter mile away, could see the surfboat floating upside down, cresting high on the waves then dropping out of view in the trough. The exhausted crew hung onto the boat's lifelines.

Captain Kiah, realizing his crew was too exhausted to right the boat, told the men they would drift to the lee side of a point on the shore, then in calmer shallower water they could right, bail the boat and mount another attempt. Several times a wave breaking over the boat scattered the men but they were all wearing their cork jackets and were able to get back to the boat. Unfortunately, it took over an hour to reach the calmer water.

The captain and crew of the *Magruder*, fearful their vessel was going to soon break up from the constant onslaught from the waves, looked on in horror as their rescuers were tossed about by the huge seas.

Captain Kiah shouted over the roar of the waves and storm to encourage the men to hold out and reminded them of their wives and children depending on them.

Unfortunately, the cold was too much for them and the men one by one succumbed to hypothermia and slipped away into the icy cold water. This occurred in view of the crew of the *Magruder* but they were helpless to lend assistance.

Mr. Samuel McFarland, alerted to the shore by his barking dogs, looked over the cliff and saw a small boat drifting towards shore. Unaware the Life Saving boat was out he ran to the Life Saving Service station but found them gone. Mr. McFarland ran the distance to the Point aux Barques Lighthouse and notified Lightkeeper Shaw of the boat drifting towards shore.

The two men raced to the beach. The empty surfboat had grounded in the shallow water. They found Captain Kiah, more dead than not. He was standing, supported by a root from a fallen tree, incoherent, frozen, swollen, and blacken of face. He was making a walking motion yet his feet were not moving. He had spent over three and a half hours in cold, unforgiving Lake Huron.

The two men took the Captain to the Life Saving station. They reported that he kept mumbling about his men and their bravery. The bodies of the surfmen drifted to shore and were found within a half mile from the station. Captain Kiah later credited the fact that his men were hot and exhausted from rowing and the cold water affected them more quickly than it did him.

Months later Captain Jerome G. Kiah and his crew were presented medals for their heroic attempts to save the lives of the crew of the *Magruder*.

Ironically, tragically and sadly, the *Magruder*, with its crew of men women and children floated free of the reef with minimal damage. The six lifesavers froze to death and their captain was left physically and mentally depleted for nothing.

# THE LAST VOYAGE OF THE YACHT GUNILDA

**T**he turn of the century was a period of contrasts in America. There were many very poor people and a few ultra wealthy. Many of those who invested in the growing oil industry lost everything they had, but a few became rich beyond their wildest dreams.

The extremely rich built huge extravagant mansions, each trying to outdo one another. They filled their homes with artwork and artifacts from around the world, and their social gatherings were the envy of the masses. The extremely rich didn't limit their extravagance to their mansions. They built private rail cars so they could travel throughout the country in the lap of luxury. It wasn't long before the rich turned their attention to yachts.

The yachts of the wealthy were as luxurious and as well appointed as their homes. They were floating palaces. One such yacht belonged to William Harkness. At the turn of the century, Mr. Harkness was one of the wealthiest men in the world, an original investor in what became known as Standard Oil. His yacht had to be bigger and better than any around. He purchased the yacht *Gunilda* and it became the flagship of the New York Yacht Club.

**113**

*The luxury ship* Gunilda. *From the collections of the Port Huron Museum.*

The *Gunilda* was built in Leith, Scotland in 1897. The magnificent vessel was 195-feet in length with a beam of almost 25-feet. The steel hulled ship drew 12-feet, 6 inches and was capable of 14 knots. Onboard the ship was fitted out for a king, nothing but the best and most opulent was good enough. The vessel sported polished mahogany brightwork, gold leafing, and shining brass on her white painted hull. The ship was sailed and maintained by a crew of 20.

One of Mr. Harkness's greatest pleasures was traveling on the *Gunilda*. The vessel had visited many American and foreign ports but during the summers of 1910 and 1911 the owner wanted to explore the Great lakes. The magnificent ship created a stir where ever it stopped along the lakes. A gleaming white ship, almost 200-feet long coming off the lake into a Great Lake port, would cause a commotion even today.

The Captain Corkum and crew of the *Gunilda* sailed the beautiful craft the length of Lake Ontario, through the Welland Canal into Lake Erie, through Lake Erie passing by Detroit and up into Lake Huron. Next was the long voyage up Lake Huron and into the Saint Marys River and then to lock through at Sault Ste. Marie into Lake Superior. Their destination was the pristine waters of the north shore of Lake Superior.

Traveling almost 200 miles across Lake Superior and stopping at some very desolate outposts along the way, Mr. Harkness, his family and two guests wanted to go into Nipigon where they heard the fishing was fantastic.

Captain Corkum, a cautious man and concerned with the safety of his passengers and the beautiful craft he was entrusted with, suggested that they hire a local pilot to guide the *Gunilda* through the maze of islands into the town of Rossport on Nipigon Bay.

Mr. Harkness, always one to save a few cents, at first declined but relented and the captain set sail to the village of Jackfish to seek a person familiar with the local water.

When Harkness heard the $15.00 charge for the guide, he adamantly refused to pay such an outrageous price. Everyone was always trying to take advantage of him, he thought.

He had a captain and crew, they had charts, why should he pay extra for someone else to pilot the *Gunilda* to a port. Mr. Harkness ordered Captain Corkum to take the ship to port and to hurry so they could get good dockage.

Captain Corkum protested that he feared their United States charts for the area were not accurate, but Mr. Harkness had made up his mind. Captain Corkum himself took the wheel to sail the gleaming *Gunilda* to Rossport.

On August 29, 1911 the ship departed Jackfish Bay for the 25 mile cruise to Rossport. The trip would take the Harkness yacht through the

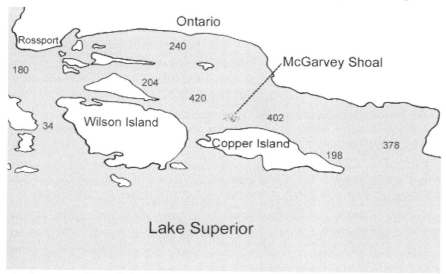

*A close up view of the area where the* Gunilda *grounded on McGarvey Shoal. The numbers indicate the depths in feet.*

Jackfish Channel into the open water of Lake Superior. The vessel would then enter the Schreiber Channel separating the mainland and Copper Island. The depths in the channel were as deep as 402-feet in places.

McGarvey shoal is a hard rock pinnacle which rises up from 280-feet of water until it is only 3-feet below the surface of the water of Nipigon Bay. The shoal, not shown on Captain Corkum's United States charts, loomed out of sight to the captain until the majestic ship steamed up onto McGarvey Shoal.

Fortunately, no one onboard the vessel was injured when the beautiful ship rode up on the shoal so hard that 80-feet of her gleaming white hull rested above the water's surface.

Mr. Harkness, being impetuous, and in an attempt to save a buck had cost himself plenty. He immediately ordered a yawl lowered and motored to Rossport to call his insurance company.

The rest of the *Gunilda* passengers were later transported to shore and taken to the Rossport Inn.

The *Gunilda*, the crown jewel of the New York Yacht Club, laid hard aground, her bow with its gilded bowsprit shined in the summer sun high above the water.

The insurance company contacted the largest tug in the area and requested it go to the aid of the stranded yacht. Several days later the tug, *James Waylan*, arrived on site from Port Arthur, some 100 miles to the west. The tug was towing a barge to use in salvaging the luxury yacht.

The tug's captain, known to be a respected and capable sailor, surveyed the situation. He suggested that another barge be sent from Port Arthur to assist with the operation.

He wanted to secure a barge on either side of the *Gunilda* with a rope sling from one barge to the other passing beneath the yacht. This arrangement would allow the *James Waylan* to pull the *Gunilda* backwards off the shoal and be supported by the barges. If the vessel were to roll to port or starboard she would be supported by the sling and not roll over. The sling arrangement would also support the *Gunilda* in the event she had sustained some undiscovered damage to the hull. If the ship started taking on water once she was off the shoal, there was nothing that could be done but race for shallow water.

Mr. Harkness, a multimillionaire, again felt he was being taken advantage of. He thought everybody was out to take his money. Mr. Harkness refused to wait for or pay for another barge to be brought from

Port Arthur. He demanded his yacht be pulled off the shoal with the tug so he could continue on his voyage.

The crew of the *James Waylan* rigged a harness at the stern of the yacht and attached to that the towing hawser which ran to the tug. Against his better judgment, the captain put the tug to forward and slowly took out the slack in the line. Once the line was nearly taut, the captain called for ahead full. The line snapped out of the water under the strain of the tug and the grounded *Gunilda*.

The yacht at first didn't budge, but with the persistence of the powerful *James Waylan* the 195-foot luxury yacht began to slowly back off McGarvey Shoal. As the ship slid free of its perch, she took on a severe list to starboard.

Within minutes of being released from the shoal, the magnificent *Gunilda* slipped beneath the surface of Nipigon Bay. The yacht that had turned so many heads as she entered ports around the world slowly sank down 280-feet to the bottom.

The barge and sling arrangement would have prevented the catastrophe, but Mr. Harkness was in too big of a hurry and too cheap to call for the second barge.

# THE WHITE STAR IS BURNING!

**F**ire onboard a ship is frightening. If the fire cannot be extinguished, the only place for the crew and passengers are the lifeboats, or if the lifeboats were consumed, they were left only one option, the water. But, not all fires occur at sea. The steamship *White Star* met its fate March 9, 1901, during winter lay up at Port Huron along the St. Clair River. The 136-foot, 378 ton vessel was preparing to begin it's 27th year on the lakes.

For the previous two weeks, Captains A. E. Slyfield and L.L. Slyfield were busy supervising the carpenters making repairs to their boat, the *White Star*. They looked forward to another season aboard the ship and hoped it would be a profitable, uneventful season. Their ship had met with enough misfortune in the past.

Just a few years earlier, while at dock in Port Huron, the *White Star* had caught fire and the cabin was completely consumed before it was extinguished. Prior to that, while the *White Star* was at Toledo, the ship had again caught fire, burning to the water line, but it was rebuilt to sail again.

A watchman at the Pere Marquette Railroad Yard was first to see the flames.

White Star---X

As he walked along the tracks checking the railcars, he saw a glow in the sky in the direction of the river. He didn't think much of it at first until he walked around a box car and saw flames leaping from the stern of a ship at the river. He ran to the office and called in an alarm to the fire department.

Captain A. E. Slyfield, who lived in Port Huron, was awakened at 2:00 in the morning by the ringing telephone. Sleepily he answered, a bit upset at being awakened at such an hour. The frantic voice on the other end told him something he didn't want to hear; his ship, the *White Star*, was on fire.

The alarm sounded at the Port Huron Fire Department and firemen scrambled to hitch the horses to the wagons and race to the wharf. When they arrived, they found the entire aft section of the ship ablaze, casting an eerie orange glow to the night sky.

The firefighters skillfully set their hoses and soon trained several streams on the ship. With the water focused on the stern, the firefighters were gaining in their fight.

Suddenly their hoses went dry. Not a drop of water came from the nozzle.

The aft of the *White Star* was soon again fully engulfed and the fire was spreading. The flames traveled below decks, igniting the forecastle and bow. Flames leaped from every port of the ship.

Captain Slyfield, upon his arrival, surveyed the situation. It was a scene he had witnessed before, although this time he saw his ship completely engulfed in flames.

The flames were spreading and there wasn't any water coming from the fire hoses. He knew there was only one thing to do. He gave the order to scuttle the ship. Intentionally sink the ship allowing the river to put out the flames.

The firemen quickly put about with axes, chopping holes in the wood hull of the *White Star*. The ship slowly listed to the starboard, then settled in the water of the St. Clair River extinguishing the flames.

The origin of the fire which took the *White Star* was never determined, it could have been intentionally set or it could have been a result of the construction. But unlike the two previous fires which struck the ship, the *White Star* would not be rebuilt.

This was the end of the line for the *White Star*. Her engine and boilers were salvaged, but the rest of the *White Star* was abandoned to the river.

The ship could have been saved if only the flow of water to the fire hoses had not stopped.

# THE WHITE STAR IS BURNING!

When the water from the fire hoses slowed to nothing, firemen raced back across the railroad tracks, along the length of the empty hoses. What they found would be funny if it wasn't so tragic. The hoses, as they lay across the railroad tracks, had been cut in two by a passing locomotive.

# THE PASSENGER SHIP CHRISTOPHER COLUMBUS

**T**he history of the Great Lakes is filled with many unusual events and unique watercraft. Arguably some of the most unusual ships to sail the inland seas were those designed by Captain Alexander McDougall. His designs remain known as "whalebacks."

The whalebacks were cigar shaped vessels with cone shaped ends. The bow of the whaleback was raised above the surface resembling a pig's snout and many referred to the boats as pigboats.

The advantage of the design was that the ships could be built quickly and less expensively than their traditional counterparts. The design of the ship also allowed the ship to operate in heavy seas at a faster speed. Their downfall was that they could not be adapted to improved unloading techniques.

During the time period of 1889 until 1898, 43 whaleback designed vessels were built. That included 19 steamers, 23 barges and the *Christopher Columbus*.

As unusual in appearance as the whalebacks were, the most unique of the whalebacks was the vessel *Christopher Columbus*. Captain McDougall designed and built the *Christopher Columbus* as a passenger ship.

X---Christopher Columbus

*The* Christopher Columbus *at sea. Photograph courtesy of the Muskegon County Museum.*

The *Christopher Columbus* was the only whaleback design constructed for passenger service, which made her quite unique; unique and also very popular.

Launched in 1892, in time to carry passengers to the World's Fair in Chicago, the ship was a huge success. The *Christopher Columbus* ran from Chicago to the World's Fair site at Jackson Park, a distance of only six miles, but the trip was a pleasure to all. The *Christopher Columbus* carried more than 2,000,000 passengers in 1893.

At the conclusion of the fair, the *Christopher Columbus* was put on the Chicago to Milwaukee run. There were other ships operating between the two cities but the *Christopher Columbus* was the favorite on the 100 mile voyage.

The most unusual of the whalebacks, the *Christopher Columbus* sailed until 1931 when she was laid up awaiting a 1936 scrapping. But, before the *Christopher Columbus* had concluded her illustrious career, the very unique ship was involved in a very unique incident.

*The "whaleback"* Colby *at the Soo Locks. From the Bayliss Public Library.*

Twenty-year-old William Steinberg of Milwaukee was waiting to board the *Christopher Columbus* for the trip to Chicago. He was anxious to get there and visit his older sister, since she had just been married.

"Mother, I am going to sail this time on the big *Christopher Columbus*. Can't you come down to the dock and see the boat sail?" William asked his mother. But household chores prevented her attending the sail.

On June 30, 1917 the *Christopher Columbus* took on passengers in preparation for the return trip to Chicago. Once the 563 passengers and crew had boarded, the *Christopher Columbus* cast off her mooring lines and two tugs, the *Welcome* and the *Knights Templar* took her in tow.

The procedure for that 4:30 pm departure was going to be the same as the ships had done on other trips out of Milwaukee. The tugs, one at the aft of the ship as the pulling tug and the other at the bow for steerage, would pull the *Christopher Columbus* backwards down the Milwaukee

*The* Christopher Columbus. *The Bayliss Public Library.*

River to the point where the river intersected with the Menomonee River. There, the steerage tug at the bow of the *Christopher Columbus*, would release its line and allow the current of the river to swing the passenger ship around. The *Christopher Columbus* would then proceed out of Milwaukee harbor under her own power into Lake Michigan.

On this occasion, Captain Moody, Master of the *Christopher Columbus* for 13 years, was concerned. The rain swollen Milwaukee River was high and it gave him concern that the *Christopher Columbus* might have trouble passing under some of the bridges. An order was issued to the tugs to proceed slowly.

Onboard the *Christopher Columbus*, passengers crowded the upper decks waving their goodbyes to Milwaukee.

As planned, the tug *Welcome* took the whaleback's stern providing the propulsion and the *Knights Templar* at the passenger ships bow provided steerage.

At a predetermined position, the *Welcome* pulled the *Christopher Columbus* stern slightly across the river and the *Knights Templar* released its line to the ship.

But the river's current, stronger than usual from the previous rains, seemed to Captain Moody to be forcing the *Christopher Columbus* bow around faster than expected.

# THE PASSENGER SHIP CHRISTOPHER COLUMBUS

As the *Christopher Columbus* swung around, Captain Moody saw that the bow, typical of all whalebacks extending out high above the waters surface and swinging faster than usual might reach over the rivers bank. If it were to reach over the bank too much it might strike something on shore.

"Get Back!" the captain bellowed into a megaphone to the passengers frolicking on the *Christopher Columbus* bow.

Captain Moody ordered the wheel to starboard in an attempt to slow the swing of the ship. When that showed no effect, he rang for reverse full.

The *Christopher Columbus,* bow continued to swing to port near the industrial buildings along the shore, until the port bow struck a support leg of a 100-foot tall storage tower, filled with 250,000 gallons of water.

The tower crashed down onto the upper deck of the *Christopher Columbus*, where many of the ship's passengers had assembled. The steel frame of the water tower smashed into the wood cabin work of the ship destroying the bridge and instantly killing many of the passengers. Passengers and crew below decks in the salon were killed or injured when the water tank and deluge of water crashed through the upper deck.

*The damaged* Christopher Columbus *moored in Milwaukee after its collision with a water tower. From the photographic collection of the Port Huron Museum.*

Passengers and crew alike chose to jump from the ship into the river and swim for safety. Moans and cries came from the twisted mass of metal and splintered wood. Blood ran off the decks into the river.

Of the 563 passengers and crew aboard the *Christopher Columbus*, 16 were killed and at least twenty were severely injured. The *Christopher Columbus* was repaired and sailed for another 14 years without incident.

After several hours of waiting for their son to come home, Mr. Steinberg of Milwaukee went to the site of the wrecked *Christopher Columbus* to look for his son.

Young William was nowhere to be found. Mr. Steinberg reluctantly went to the morgue. There he was shown the twelve yet unidentified bodies from the accident. As each marble table was slid out from the shelving, Mr. Steinberg had to force himself to look. Mr. Steinberg wanted to find out about his son but he didn't want to look.

Eleven slabs were pulled out, the twelfth held William Steinberg.

Mrs. Steinberg wailed at the news. She repeatedly said, "Why didn't I go to the dock and see him off?"

Despite her illustrious career, the *Christopher Columbus*, pride of Alexander McDougall, could never shake the dubious reputation of being the only ship on the Great Lakes to run into an onshore water tank.

# THE DISAPPEARANCE OF THE INKERMAN AND CERISOLES

**G**reat Lake ship disappearances are nothing new. Most likely long since before recorded history vessels were lost on the lakes. Native Americans sailed out on the lakes in primitive canoes never to return. Some vessel losses have become more familiar with the public while others remain somewhat obscure, known mostly to Great Lakes historians. Many of the details of the loss of the *Inkerman* and *Cerisoles* have been lost to history. But, to this day, the disappearance of the two vessels remains a mystery.

During World War I, all available shipyards were called into service to build the weapons of war. The French government issued a request for bids for twelve minesweepers.

The steel vessels were to be 143-feet in length and 23-feet in beam. The ships would be employed in locating and destroying enemy mines in European harbors. They had to be built sturdy enough to withstand the nearby concussions of exploding mines as they were detonated.

In February 1918 the Canadian Car and Foundry Company in Fort William, Ontario was building railroad cars but the owners bid on and received the contract to build the twelve ships for the French government.

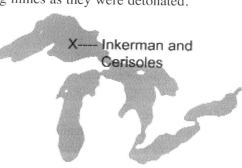

X----Inkerman and Cerisoles

*The French minesweeper photographed in varying stages of construction. From the collection of the Thunder Bay Museum, Thunder Bay, Ontario.*

The twelve minesweepers were to be named after victorious military battles from French History. The names selected were *Bautzen*, *Cerisoles*, *Inkerman*, *Leoben*, *Lutzen*, *Malakoff*, *Mantoue*, *Navarin*, *Palestro*, *Saint Georges*, *Sebastopol*, and *Senef.*

All twelve ships had to be completed by October 1918, a feat which would tax the skills and endurance of the workmen at the Canadian Car and Foundry Company but a challenge they were ready to take on. The October deadline was to allow the vessels time to transit the length of Lake Superior and lock down into Lake Huron. The minesweepers would then travel the length of Lake Huron, Lake St. Clair, down to Lake Erie. At the east end of Lake Erie they would take the Welland Canal into Lake Ontario. After crossing Lake Ontario they would enter the seaway at Montreal and make for the Atlantic Ocean. The ships then would need to cross the ocean for final delivery. All of the travel had to be done prior to the waterways freezing over.

Construction on the first of the twelve ships began almost immediately after the contract was signed. By July of 1918 the first of the ships was launched and five others were completed and launched in short order.

The ships were subjected to sea trials on Lake Superior then set out for delivery. The minesweepers were fitted with two 120 mm guns, manned by a 38 member French crew and an experienced Canadian pilot and then departed.

As each ship was completed, another was started. The workers at the Canadian Car and Foundry Company worked around the clock to fulfill the contract. The last three minesweepers were completed in late October and readied to depart for Europe.

The three ships, the *Sebastopol*, the *Inkerman*, and the *Cerisoles*, cleared Fort William on November 23, 1918 under the command of French Captain Leclerc aboard the *Sebastopol*.

The fleet of three departed Fort William, and while giving plenty of distance between them and the northern tip of Isle Royale, a fall storm

*The minesweepers were 143-feet in length and 23-feet in beam. From the collection of the Thunder Bay Museum, Thunder Bay, Ontario.*

*The minesweeper's deck gun on the bow. From the collection of the Thunder Bay Museum, Thunder Bay, Ontario.*

developed from the southwest. The wind blew violently and the horizontal snow limited visibility, a typical Lake Superior late November blizzard.

Captain Leclerc and the Canadian pilots communicated by wireless and decided to divert from their straight course to Sault Saint Marie and turned into the storm to follow the southern shore of the lake along to Whitefish Point. This way they would be somewhat sheltered by the coast.

While making the maneuver, the *Sebastopol* lost sight of the *Inkerman* and the *Cerisoles* in the blizzard. The radio operator aboard the *Sebastopol* repeatedly tried to establish radio contact with the other two ships but if the *Inkerman* and the *Cerisoles* were receiving his message, they never responded.

Captain Leclerc ordered the *Sebastopol* to continue since he felt the two missing vessels were new with experienced sailors and they would sail through the storm and the three would rendezvous at the locks.

# THE DISAPPEARANCE OF THE INKERMAN & CERISOLES

Arriving at Sault Ste. Marie on November 26, the *Sebastopol* moored and awaited the arrival of the *Inkerman* and the *Cerisoles*. Three days later the two minesweepers had not arrived.

Captain Leclerc notified the United States Coast Guard of the overdue vessels. The Coast Guard searched the southern coast of Lake Superior while a private tug, hired by Captain Leclerc, set off to search the north shore.

After days of searching the coasts, dotted with islands and indented with coves, and communicating with freighters on the lookout for the two vessels or wreckage of them, nothing was found. No lifeboats, no wreckage, no bodies, nothing that would indicate what had happened to the *Inkerman* and the *Cerisoles*.

Two brand new 143-foot steel minesweepers and eighty men had disappeared into Lake Superior.

Theories of the cause of the loss of the *Inkerman* and the *Cerisoles* abounded. Everyone had a reason for the disappearance of the vessels.

One theory was that the ships were built so quickly that the sinking was the fault of the Canadian Car and Foundry Company. It was said the ship's steel plates were partially assembled with wood pegs. The wood pegs were later removed and replaced with rivets. A theory presented stated the pegs were left in and the ships basically fell apart. The theory was quickly discredited.

Another thought was that the two military vessels were secretly transferred to the United States for use in its navy. This theory was vehemently denied by the United States, France and the Canadian Car and Foundry Company.

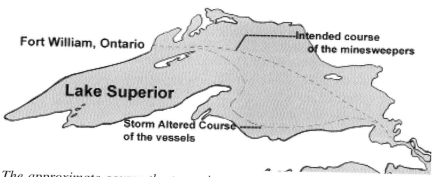

*The approximate course the two minesweepers would have followed had the weather been good, and the approximate southern course the vessels might have followed in the storm.*

*A view of the cabin structure of one of the minesweepers. From the collection of the Thunder Bay Museum, Thunder Bay, Ontario.*

In 1929 a United States Survey Vessel was charting the bottom of Lake Superior, using an early echo sounder to record the depths. The captain sat up and took notice of the echo sounder. It had been reading depths of 600- to 750-feet when it suddenly began to record lesser depths of 328-feet, 214-feet, 114-feet. Thinking that the machine had malfunctioned, the captain ordered the vessel to backtrack its course to check that section of Lake Superior again.

The echo sounder again recorded the same depths, and even shallower depths were found. At one location the depths were between 33- and 16-feet deep! A previously undiscovered rock mountain jutted up over 700-feet from the bottom of Lake Superior. The mountain was located directly on the course from Thunder Bay to Sault Ste. Marie.

Could the *Inkerman* and the *Cerisoles* possibly have run onto the rocky point in the storm and been holed and quickly sunk? The vessels were equipped with wireless radios and a message could have been sent if there was time. But no radio distress calls were sent.

*One of the French minesweepers with her crew, underway on Lake Superior. From the collection of the Thunder Bay Museum, Thunder Bay, Ontario.*

The most widely accepted theory to explain the loss of the *Inkerman* and the *Cerisoles* was that the storm which ravaged the lake those days in November 1918 simply overpowered the two minesweepers. A huge wave might have crashed down on the stern of one or both of the vessels and sent them quickly to the bottom. Or possibly the two ships might have collided in the limited visibility of the blizzard.

In 1934 two men were exploring the inlets on Michipicoten Island. The island is located in the northeast corner of Lake Superior. The men went ashore at West Sand Bay where they found the skeletal remains of two men. The skeletons wore the remains of what looked like Navy uniforms and French military identification tags.

The two men placed the remains in a wood fish box and buried it above the lake's waterline. They took the tags and sent them in to the authorities.

Sixteen years after the disappearance of the two minesweepers, the remains of two of its crew had been found. The bodies had either been drifting in the lake for years, finally beaching on Michipicoten Island, or they might have been found and buried by a trapper who did not report it, only to be uncovered by a storm. However, the skeletons came to rest on the island and two of the missing 80 had been found.

The *Inkerman* and the *Cerisoles* were two large, brand new, steel ships. They had an experienced crew and experienced pilots who were familiar with Lake Superior, yet, the two minesweepers disappeared. There were none of the telltale signs which usually indicated the location of the loss, no debris field, only a couple of bodies, no wireless distress call, no lifeboat. Despite many attempts to locate the final resting place of the two vessels, and the sophisticated electronics now available, to this day the *Inkerman* and the *Cerisoles* have not been found!

# THE SINKING OF THE TUG BLISH

**T**he tug *Blish* was secured to the dock the last time anyone saw her, but later she was found on the bottom. Here is what happened to the tug *Blish* in 1862.

The tug was tied up at Algonac, Michigan along the St. Clair River while her engineer prepared her for the day. He left for a few hours and when he returned the tug was sitting on the bottom.

The sinking could be the result of any number of reasons. Maybe she had struck a submerged object the last time she was out and opened a small hole. Or possibly some seams of her wood planked hull had sprung allowing water to enter the hull and maybe the packing around the shaft had shifted. The cause wouldn't be known until the tug could be raised.

A wrecking crew was brought in. A diver was sent down to look for obvious damage. The damage would need to be patched before anything else was done. No damage could be seen. The salvage crew set to work with pumps until she slowly came to the surface.

The tug, once submerged, had sustained water damage to her machinery. A costly and extensive cleanup job lay

X---Tug Blish

before the owners of the tug, but first the cause of the sinking had to be determined so it wouldn't happen again.

A close inspection showed that while the engineer was onboard, he started a small secondary steam engine used to operate deck equipment. He was using it to draw water into the boiler in preparation of building up steam for the day.

Unfortunately, the engineer had not noticed that a valve on the bottom of the boiler was not closed. He left the vessel and the pump filled the tug with water until she sank!

The engineer was fired.

# CAPTAIN MATTISON AND THE D.L. FILER

**T**he 159-foot *Tempest* steamed out of Buffalo Harbor with two barges in tow. The barge *Interlaken* was destined for Toledo and the steamer and barge *D.L. Filer* were filled with coal bound for Saugatuck, Michigan on lower Lake Michigan, a journey which would cover a distance of over 800 miles.

The trip was nothing out of the ordinary for the old steamer, *Tempest*, this 1916 season being her 44th year on the Great Lakes. She had seen a lot of miles, a lot of cargo and a lot of weather. The barges were the 23 year old *Interlaken,* and the *D.L. Filer* was in her 45th season and had weathered her share on the lakes as well. The *Interlaken* and the *D.L. Filer* were built as schooners and sailed the lakes until steam vessels became more cost effective and rendered the old sailing craft of little use other than a barge.

The *Interlaken* and *D.L. Filer* would spend the rest of their careers being loaded and off loaded and pulled from port to port. They would never again raise their sails, feel the acceleration as the sails filled, they would never again sail under their own power. Their era in history was passing.

In mid October, 1916 the ships sailed out into Lake Erie under clear

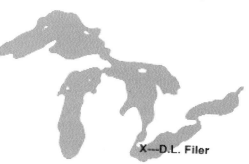

X---D.L. Filer

skies, but there was a storm brewing. It was a storm that to this day is still called "Black Friday", Friday October 20, 1916, when a severe weather system took aim at Lake Erie and unleashed its full fury on the ships and sailors.

Crossing Lake Erie, the *Tempest* towed the *D.L. Filer* towards Saugatuck. As the three vessels neared Toledo, Ohio, the *D.L. Filer* was anchored off Bar Point, near the entrance to the Detroit River, while the *Tempest* with the *Interlaken* in tow, steamed into Toledo to discharge the barge and pick up another. The *Tempest* and her new barge would rendezvous with the *D.L. Filer* and both barges would be towed to Saugatuck.

Unfortunately for Captain John Mattison, Master of the *D.L. Filer* and its crew of six, the Black Friday storm was about to bore down on Lake Erie and the old schooner was in the way.

The schooner, anchored by the bow and stern, strained at its anchor chain as the winds increased and the waves began to grow. As the storm increased in intensity and the winds grew from a terrible 50 mile per hour wind to a horrendous 70 miles per hour in velocity, the *D.L. Filer's* anchor lost its bite and began to drag along the bottom.

*An artist's concept of Captain Mattison and Oscar Johansson clinging to the rigging of the sunken* D.L. Filer.

About 8:00 pm, Captain Mattison called the crew together and yelled to them over the shrieking of the wind to be prepared for sudden action if it became necessary. Over the roar of the storm, the snapping of the forward anchor chain was heard.

The schooner was helpless in the storm. The *D.L. Filer* was blown off position before the wind. The ship dragged her stern anchor, the crew praying it would grab.

The *D.L. Filer* was thrown about by the furious waves. With no engine or sails, no means of propulsion, the vessel was at the will of the angry lake. The ship was swept into the trough of the waves and rolled violently. Then an enormous wave smashed down on the ship and she began to settle by the stern.

The conditions were so terrible that the crew all knew leaving the ship in the yawl meant certain death. One man ran to the foremast and started climbing the rope ladder. The rest of the crew knew Lake Erie was notoriously shallow and that if the *D.L. Filer* were to founder, the upper masts might remain above the angry lake. The crew climbed as high as they could up the masts.

The six sailors climbed to the masthead as Captain Mattison remained on the deck. As the *D.L. Filer*, being beaten by the seas and wind, slowly settled to the bottom, Captain Mattison took to the rope ladder.

Waist deep in the wind whipped lake, Captain Mattison struggled to climb higher, but the rope ladder came loose from its moorings from the weight of seven men clinging to it. The captain threw a leg around the mast and held fast to a rope loosely swinging near him. The rest of the crew were all flung into the raging sea. They tried to swim back to the ship but all but one man were quickly blown out of sight.

Oscar Johansson, weighted down by his oilskins, with strength from some unknown source, struggled against the turmoil back to the mast. Now only Oscar and the captain remained. And they were not sure how long they could hang on.

The two men clung to the mast, the raging lake just a few feet below them, their weakening voices barely heard over the waves and storm. The men were freezing in the cold rain and winds, their fingers stiffening with cold. After three long torturous hours Oscar yelled to the captain, "Its all up with me, I can't hang on much longer!"

"Hang on Oscar!" the captain yelled. "This sea can't scare a Norseman!"

Oscar took a tighter grip and buried his face in his oilskins, trying to shield it from the biting wind-blown spray.

Twice throughout the night Mr. Johansson began to slip but both times Captain Mattison was able to grab him and bring him back to the mast.

In the early hours of the morning, the storm had subsided and the two men had been clinging to the foremast for almost nine hours. They were physically and mentally exhausted. The lights of a freighter were sighted, The men yelled and waved but the ship was two miles away and the men weren't seen. Hope turned to despair.

Another freighter was seen but it too passed by without seeing the two freezing men.

At a dock in Detroit, the D & C Navigation Company's liner, passenger ship *Western States* was scheduled to depart the day the storm struck Lake Erie, but the company, aware of conditions on the lake, ordered the ship held at Detroit. The following day the storm had subsided and the *Western States* was able to depart.

The *Western States* sailed south on the Detroit River nearing Lake Erie. Conditions were still rough but the worst of the Black Friday storm had passed. As the passenger ship rounded Bar Point, a lookout in the pilothouse spotted a strange sight. It was two masts of a sunken schooner. Captain Robinson was told of the sighting. He took up the glasses (binoculars) and scanned the area. It looked like there were two men in the rigging. "Take it closer," Captain Robinson ordered the wheelsman.

After the two freighters had passed without sighting the men, Oscar Johansson and Captain Mattison, weakened from exhaustion and cold, were saddened and ready to give up. The lake had all but defeated them. Both men were ready to cash it in, just slip into the lake and give up. Then the *Western States* came into view.

Captain Mattison wearily waved his cap to the ship and the *Western States* sounded its whistle, letting the men know they had been seen.

The big passenger ship slowly came closer, careful not to run aground on the Bar Point shoal. Stopping about 1,000-feet from the distressed men in the rigging, the ship anchored. Captain Robinson ordered a boat lowered away.

As the five men in the lifeboat pulled at the oars, Oscar Johansson, unable to hold on any longer, fell from the mast into the lake. He never resurfaced. Captain Mattison looked on but this time he couldn't help him as he had throughout the night.

Captain Mattison jumped from the mast into the lake. His oilskins threatening to pull him down as he swam towards the lifeboat.

The captain, half frozen and exhausted, was taken to the passenger ship. He was warmed by the stewards and taken to a stateroom, where he slept until the *Western States* arrived at Cleveland.

Lake Erie had destroyed the *D.L. Filer*, killed six of crew but, while Captain Mattison, Master of the old schooner mourned for his men, he had beaten the lake. He took all that the lake could throw at him and he survived.

# THE MYSTERIOUS SINKING OF TUGBOAT SACHEM

**I**t was December 18, 1950. The weather had been unusually cold and Lake Erie was already beginning to ice over. But the tugboat *Sachem* was being readied for departure.

At 7:00 am, the 71-foot tugboat *Sachem*, owned by the Dunbar & Sullivan Dredging Company, left Buffalo, New York en-route to Dunkirk, New York. There she would pick up a tow, a barge with a dredging derrick, and return to Buffalo. The round trip would cover approximately 70 miles.

Shortly after the *Sachem* powered out of the Buffalo Harbor, she passed an inbound steamer and exchanged the customary whistle signals. The tug then set a course to the southwest towards Dunkirk on Lake Erie's south shore.

Onboard the *Sachem* was a crew of twelve including Captain Hector Church from Lincoln Park, Michigan, First Engineer George Burns, Deckhand Francis Dugan, Oiler Charles Roberts, and Deckhand Russ McKinney, all from Michigan.

Members of the *Sachem* crew from New York were; Deckhand Tom Shine, Second Engineer Frank Reynolds, Mate Laverne Graf, and Oilers John

Tugboat Sachem X

**145**

*The tug* Sachem. *Courtesy of the Lower Lake Marine Historical Society.*

Farrell and Tom Boice. The cook, Dan Ryan, was from Ohio and the twelfth man onboard the *Sachem* was Hans Von Frankenstein, a consulting Diesel Engineer from Winnetka, Illinois.

The *Sachem* was built in 1907 at the old Ohio Basin Slip. The steel tug had recently been converted from steam to diesel propulsion and Hans Von Frankenstein was aboard to make tests on the new propulsion system.

By late afternoon on December 18, 1950, concern began to mount, for the Dunbar & Sullivan Dredging Company's tug *Sachem* had not reached its destination of Dunkirk, New York.

Since the *Sachem* was not radio equipped, the tug could not communicate with shore side facilities. Possibly the tug was experiencing mechanical problems but could not inform the company of the delay.

The Coast Guard sent out a message to all ships in the area requesting information of sightings of the *Sachem*. The steamer *Venus* said they had seen the tug earlier that morning near Waverly Shoal Buoy shortly after the tug departed Buffalo. But there were not any other sightings of the tug. The *Sachem* was officially declared missing and a general alarm was issued for all ships to watch for the tug.

As the news of the missing tug reached Buffalo and Detroit, cities where most of the crew resided, many Great Lake sailors saw no need for concern. Ships sometimes broke down and drifted off course. The tug probably had not been seen because the ship traffic on the lake this late in the season was minimal.

Another theory which was spoken of amongst sailors was that the tug, newly converted to diesel, had mechanical difficulties and had pulled into some remote cove along the Lake Erie south shore, or that maybe she had drifted to the more desolate north Canadian shore. It might be a day or two before the ship could be repaired or until a crewman walked along the shore to a town for assistance.

In either case, most seamen agreed the *Sachem* would be seen or heard from soon. After all, this wasn't the late 1800's when ship disappearances were commonplace, this was the 1950's!

As the day progressed to night and the tug still had not been heard from, concern turned to fear for the men of the *Sachem*. Preparations were made for a search of the east portion of southern Lake Erie, the area following the tug's course and where the tug most likely might be sheltering. The search would then be broadened to include the entire lake.

Several Coast Guard rescue boats were dispatched to search the lake and the 180-foot Naval Reserve Patrol Boat, *PC-1208* from Buffalo left its base at 10:00 pm to join the search.

At noon on Tuesday, the day following the disappearance of the *Sachem*, the *PC-1208* returned. Lieutenant Edward Tucker, commanding officer of the ship and director of the search operations and all vessels involved in the search, felt confident that the ship had not met with a tragedy.

"The tug is probably docked safely somewhere between Buffalo and Detroit," the Lieutenant said. "The entire lake was searched between the two cities without success. Visibility was good and there appeared little chance the craft had foundered."

Since the search ships had not discovered a debris field and air planes in the search did not see an oil slick on the surface, many veteran lake men were confident the *Sachem* was sheltering somewhere. They argued that a 72-foot steel vessel with a crew of twelve couldn't sink without a trace. There was always something floating on the surface, lifeboats, flotsam, life preservers or bodies to tell the tale of a ship which was sent to the bottom.

*The United States Coast Guard vessel* Acacia *was active in the search for the missing* Sachem. *From the Hugh Clark Great Lakes Photograph Collection.*

By the second day of the disappearance, the search party had grown to include the Coast Guard Cutter *Acacia* and icebreaker *Tupelo*, smaller craft from police and sheriff's departments, ground units which searched the beaches, a Coast Guard PBY which flew in from Traverse City, Michigan, other airplanes from Selfridge Army Air Field near Detroit, airplanes from the U.S. Naval Air Station at Niagara Falls, New York, a Sheriff's Department helicopter, and the Ontario Provincial Police. The tug *Sachem* was still not found.

The search for the missing tug *Sachem* and her crew of twelve became the most extensive and broad search ever on Lake Erie and possibly the Great Lakes.

The weather turned foul by Friday, December 22. A cold rain fell, freezing immediately on whatever it landed, snow squalls invaded the area and there were heavy seas on the lake. The airplanes were grounded and only the large ships could continue the search. Yet even the large Coast Guard vessels were hampered in their efforts by ice fields forming on the lake.

# THE MYSTERIOUS SINKING OF TUGBOAT SACHEM

Hope of finding the tug and crew was diminishing. The talk on the docks and in the wharfside bars had shifted from the *Sachem* sheltering in a secluded cove to the ship must have come to a violent and quick end.

One theory was that the tug must have exploded without warning sending her plummeting to the bottom. The lack of survivors or lifeboats floating on the lake's surface indicated the crew did not have an opportunity to escape. Yet an exploding ship usually leaves a debris field and none had been discovered despite the extensive search.

Other veteran seamen theorized that a freak wave must have over taken the tug and sent her to the bottom. There were no reports of heavy seas, but a freak wave on the lakes, a Seiche Wave, is not unheard of.

Some Great Lake sailors put forth a theory that the tug might have encountered an ice field and attempted to plow through it but rode up on it instead. The tug, bow high on thick ice and stern low would have to back off. A tug with little freeboard aft could easily slip beneath the surface while reversing without any warning. The crew would not have had a chance to escape, which would account for no survivors or bodies being found.

The weather at the time of the disappearance did not seem to be of concern. The temperature was 23 degrees Fahrenheit, the winds blowing at 14 miles per hour from the north northwest with intermittent

*The United States Coast Guard Icebreaker* Tupelo. *From the Hugh Clark Great Lakes Photograph Collection.*

snow squalls, conditions which would make the trip uncomfortable but not impassable.

Theories and conjectures abounded but all that was known to be true was that the tug *Sachem* had left Buffalo around 7:00 am on Monday, December 18, 1950 and had not been seen or heard from since.

On December 23, five days after the disappearance, while searching for a sign of the tug *Sachem*, the United States Coast Guard Icebreaker *Tupelo* discovered an oil slick. The 15-foot wide and 40-foot long slick was located off Silver Creek, New York about 3.6 miles off shore and 11 miles northeast of Dunkirk, the *Sachem's* destination.

The *Tupelo* made sonar soundings of the lake around the oil slick and found the average depths of about 90-feet and charts indicated the lake bottom to be fairly level, but at the location of the oil slowly bubbling to the surface the soundings were only 64- to 68-feet in depth. Something was down there.

"While this evidence is not conclusive," Lieutenant Commander Marion Amos announced, "the various factors involved are enough to warrant a definite check through diving operations."

The factors that Mr. Amos referred to were the location of the oil slick on a course the tug should have followed between Buffalo and Dunkirk, an object about the size of the missing tug on the normally level bottom, and samples of the oily substance appearing to be diesel fuel. The *Sachem* had departed Buffalo with 7,000 gallons of diesel fuel in her tanks.

The owners of the tug *Sachem*, the Dunbar & Sullivan Dredging Company, told the Coast Guard that they would conduct the diving operation as soon as the weather would allow.

The search for the missing tug was called off based on the strong evidence that the object located was that of the *Sachem*.

Three young boys, playing on the ice mounds tossed up on the shore near Sunset Bay, came across something of importance. The boys, ages 5 to 8, found a green painted lifeboat washed up in the ice piled up by the waves.

The 16-foot steel lifeboat was intact except a large dent stove in near its keel. Lying in the bottom was a single orange life preserver. Stenciled on the storm battered boat was the name *Sachem*.

Law enforcement personnel and volunteers searched the surrounding area for bodies or other wreckage from the *Sachem* along the shore but turned up nothing.

After a thorough inspection by the Sheriff's Department and State Police, they determined the lifeboat had been on shore for a while, probably since the night of the disappearance. The hull contained beach sand blown in by the winds before the beach was covered by ice and snow from the recent winter storms. It is suspected that the lifeboat was overlooked during the intensive search because from the air it might have been confused with the cottage boats left along the shore.

So much evidence pointed to the object on the lake's bottom being the missing *Sachem* but it was still not known for sure. A diver had to descend to the object and verify it was the *Sachem* or some other previously unknown wreck.

On January 5, 1951 a grizzly discovery was made in two separate locations along the lake's south shore. The bodies of two men were found. The coroner was able to determine the bodies were those of the *Sachem's* cook Dan Ryan and George Burns, the ship's engineer. The *Sachem's* crew was beginning to return to shore.

On January 23, 1951 an attempt was made to dive on the object suspected to be the *Sachem*. Diver Frank Cappello, operating from a converted World War II landing craft, the *Albatross*, was slowly lowered beneath the icy waters of Lake Erie.

It was verified that the mysterious object was indeed the tugboat *Sachem*.

"I was in the dark and could see nothing," said Cappello. "I felt my way around."

Diver Cappello found the tug to be covered with a thick layer of silt making his task very difficult. His every motion stirred the silt up making it nearly impossible for him to see. But he was able to explore the pilot house and the boiler room and grasping around in the dark he felt the engine.

Diver Cappello theorized that since the tug went down in mid-morning some of the crew might have been in the forecastle, but he could not access it because the door was locked. In the search of other parts of the ship he did not find any bodies or any indication of why the ship sank. He suggested the silt around the tug would have to be removed or the tug raised to discover the cause of the sinking.

No bodies of the crew of the *Sachem* were found aboard the sunken vessel on this initial dive, but earlier that day two more bodies, identified as crew of the *Sachem*, were discovered.

Conditions and availability of equipment did not permit another dive on the *Sachem* until early June of 1951, almost seven months after the ship had slipped below the lake. Captain Finnegan of Silver Creek again directed the operation from his vessel the *Albatross*.

*The raising of the tug* Sachem. *Courtesy of the Lower Lakes Marine Historical Society.*

"Our divers have explored the tug from stem to stern and have found no trace of any of the eight bodies still unaccounted for," said Roger Cook, counsel for the Dunbar & Sullivan Dredging Company.

The *Albatross* was equipped with a compressor designed to blow away the accumulated silt. This device would be used to remove the silt covering the tug and hopefully expose the cause of the sinking.

In August of 1951 another crewman from the sunken tug *Sachem* was found. The body of Tom Boice, a deckhand aboard the *Sachem*, surfaced near the town of Brant. Seven crewmembers still remain unaccounted for. It was Tom Boice's name that was found scratched in the lifeboat. He was found only a short distance from where the lifeboat was located.

The lake would eventually give up all but four of the crew of the ill-fated tugboat *Sachem*.

The tug *Sachem* was found to be in salvageable condition and the Dunbar & Sullivan Dredging Company arranged to have the vessel raised. Once it was again on the surface, the tug was towed to Detroit where it was lifted out of the water so the hull could be inspected. The *Sachem* gave no indication why she sank and took her crew with her.

In 1952, the results of an exhaustive inquiry into the cause of the sinking of the tugboat *Sachem* and the death of her crew was made public.

They determined the cause to be the result of one of two conditions. Either the *Sachem* was overtaken by a huge wave and swamped or the ship was a victim of ice building up on the vessel and causing it to capsize.

A wave of unusually heavy proportions might have struck the ship and capsized the vessel in seconds. The Marine Board assumed in this theory that an unusually large wave was sighted to the ship's starboard. The Pilot would turn hard to starboard to meet the wave head on. And it would not be unusual for the pilot to stop the engine momentarily to slow the impact the wave would have on the ship. The *Sachem's* control was found in stop position and the rudder was hard to starboard. The windows of the wheelhouse were also found to be smashed inward.

The rogue wave theory was very plausible, but the Marine Board could not eliminate the icing theory. The weather on that day was below freezing and the waves were sufficient to send spray over the vessel. The spray might have built up a coat of ice on the cabins and pilothouse to the extent that the ship's center of gravity was adversely affected. With the additional weight of the ice on the upper structures, the *Sachem* would roll heavily in the seas. If the roll became critical, the vessel would capsize and sink.

The exact cause will never be discovered; no one lived to tell. After lying on the bottom for 10 months, the ship was raised, repaired, and put back into service by the Dunbar & Sullivan Dredging Company.

Ironically, five years after the tug *Sachem* departed Buffalo Harbor on a trip to the bottom of Lake Erie and the death of her crew, the tug returned to Buffalo. The company was awarded the contract to deepen the lower end of Buffalo Harbor and the once missing tug was back working out of Buffalo Harbor.

Forty-year-old Tom Shine told his wife as he left on December 18, 1950 that it would be his last trip of the season. "I promise I'll be home for Christmas," he told her as he was leaving their Buffalo, New York home. It was a promise he couldn't keep.

# SABOTAGE
# AT THE SOO!

**T**he two soldiers pulled the collar of their coats up against the cold damp October winds blowing in from Lake Superior. They were from Company C, of the 702nd Military Police Battalion, assigned to protect the strategically critical Soo Locks at Sault Ste. Marie, Michigan and Ontario.

It was October 7, 1941, two months to the day before the surprise attack on the United States Naval Fleet at Pearl Harbor, Hawaii. War was ravaging Europe. The newspapers were filled with articles of Adolph Hitler's Nazi forces advancing on the Soviet Russia city of Moscow. America's massive industrial complex was producing war related products for the allied forces and in anticipation of America's entrance into the war. The iron ore mined in Minnesota and Upper Michigan on the shores of Lake Superior was transported by a huge fleet of Great Lakes freighters to the steel mills on the lower lakes.

To transport cargo by ship from Lake Superior to the other Great Lakes there is only one way to go, through the St. Marys River which connects Lake Superior to Lake Huron. All ships and cargo must pass through the river. The level of

---Sault Ste. Marie

*The American Locks at Sault Ste. Marie can be seen in this aerial view. Several sections of the one mile long International Bridge are in the middle of the photograph. From the State of Michigan Archives, Lansing, Michigan.*

Lake Superior being 21-feet higher than Lake Huron required that locks be built to tame the raging rapids and raise the vessels to Lake Superior's level or down from Lake Superior to Lake Huron's level.

The war preparations required that huge amounts of the raw material pass safely through the St. Marys River. The narrow river, critical to America's future war efforts, had to be protected from possible acts of sabotage. If the locks were destroyed or even damaged, the flow of iron ore would be drastically reduced and the production of the weapons of war would be severely impaired.

More cargo had passed through the locks that year than ever before. From January to September, 82,838,697 tons was locked through, most of it was iron ore. By the end of the year it was expected that 100,000,000 tons would lock through, surpassing the old record by a huge margin.

The military presence on both the American and Canadian shores of the river was intense. Searchlights were put in place throughout the area to illuminate possible enemy aircraft, and anti-aircraft weapon installations were manned and ready for anything that might come their way. The military maintained guards at all crossings and at the locks to protect against acts of sabotage.

# SABOTAGE AT THE SOO!

*The military was ever present at the Locks to counter any possible act of sabotage. From the State of Michigan Archives, Lansing, Michigan.*

In the early hours of October 7, 1941 the soldiers stood guard on the International Bridge, a railroad bridge which crossed the St. Marys River. The International Bridge provided a railroad connection between Sault Ste. Marie, Ontario on the Canadian side and Sault Ste. Marie, Michigan in the United States.

The bridge is actually a one mile long series of bridges consisting of two swing bridges, one on the American side over the Poe Lock approach and one on the Canadian side crossing the canal to the Canadian lock. There were also several fixed spans over the rapids and a bascule, or draw bridge, which crossed the approach to the Davis and Sabin locks.

The bridges normally stayed in the open position allowing ship traffic to pass unimpeded, only closing when a train needed to cross.

At 1:30 am the soldiers spotted the headlight of a train from the Canadian side. They opened the wire gates at the bridge and took up their positions to allow the train to pass. After the locomotive, tender and 45 cars rumbled past their position and into the dark night, the soldiers heard a crumpling sound, the screeching of metal on metal and a huge splash.

The men knew the train must have fallen into the channel!

Private Ted Adseh later reported, "We heard the train hit the water and started running down the bridge right away." The two guards sprinted the 600-feet along the wet and slippery railroad ties towards the horrific sound.

*Searchlights scanned the night sky watching for enemy aircraft which might try to bomb the locks. From the Bayliss Public Library, Sault Ste. Marie, Michigan.*

When they reached the end of the Bascule they couldn't see anything, but heard someone groaning. Private Adseh shined his flashlight down towards the water and saw two trainmen hanging onto the iron beams of the bridge.

Private Adseh and Private Bellinger climbed down the twisted girders which were once the north section of the Bascule Bridge to assist the men in climbing up. With much effort and pain the two trainmen were brought to the roadway. The two, fireman Carl Zelmer and brakeman Francis Peller, were taken to the Fort Brady Hospital.

In the hours that followed the accident, military personnel and civil authorities poured over the bridge with flashlights searching for signs of sabotage. Rumors ran rampant that an enemy of the United States had destroyed the railroad bridge in an attempt to slow if not stop the flow of iron ore to the steel mills. The bridge had stood for 30 years so it had to be sabotaged. It couldn't have just fallen into the St. Marys River!

*Soldiers stood guard on the railroad bridges watching for any suspicious activity. From the State of Michigan Archives, Lansing, Michigan.*

*The Bascule Bridge crossing the approach to the Davis and Sabin locks. The massive counter weights can clearly be seen at both ends of the bridge sections. From the State of Michigan Archives, Lansing, Michigan.*

Was it an act of sabotage? Had some unknown person or persons representing an enemy to the United States rigged the bridge to collapse into the lock approach, in effect halting shipping through the two largest of the locks? An inspection of the bridge began at once and witnesses were interrogated.

Carl Zilmer told investigators that the signal lights on the bridge instructed the train to stop before it entered the Canadian side of the bridge. In a matter of minutes the signal had changed indicating a clear track. The following is Zelmer's account as reported in the *Sault Ste. Marie Evening News*.

"Happy (H.J. Willis, the Engineer) asked me if I was all set as the way was clear, and we started out on the bridge," Zilmer said. "It suddenly sounded like the engine had jumped the tracks, and the first time I knew something was wrong is when I saw the nose of the engine hit the water. The on-rush of water forced me back against the top of the cab and threw Peller against the boiler head. Both of us went clean to the bottom. After we stopped going down, Peller went out the gangway and I went out the right window, by which I had been standing." Zilmer continues, "It seemed like I would never come to the surface and when I did I was about fifty or sixty feet from the sunken bridge."

The two men swam to the bridge and clung to the girder where the soldiers found them.

The International Bridge was owned by the Canadian Pacific Railroad Company. It was originally opened in 1888.

The bridge went through many alterations during its life span, one being the construction of the Bascule Bridge in 1911.

*The two spans of the Bascule Bridge across the approach of the Davis and Sabin locks shown raising to allow a ship to pass. Courtesy of the Dawn Collection of the Bayliss Public Library, Sault Ste. Marie, Michigan.*

The Bascule Bridge was 330-feet long and spanned the 280-feet wide approach to the two largest of the four locks.

The effect the tragedy had on Great Lakes shipping was enormous. By 10:30 am there were approximately 25 downbound ore ships lying at anchor awaiting passage through the locks. While only the Davis and Sabin locks were blocked, the ships could not use the Poe or Canadian locks. Those two locks were too shallow for the fully loaded ships. The normal draft of a fully loaded ore boat is 20-feet. The Canadian lock can handle only ships which draw less than 17-feet, 4 inches and the Poe 16-feet, six inches.

It was surmised that another 50 vessels had taken on their cargo before the bridge collapsed and those ships would arrive at the locks soon. And another 50 were expected on the following day. The blockade of vessels awaiting passage through the locks was going to be tremendous.

Military officials ordered all ships not yet loaded that they could not take on so much ore that would cause them to draw more that 16-feet. That would allow them to pass through the two open locks.

In the meantime the investigation into the cause of the collapse of the bridge continued. It could have been sabotage or any number of other reasons. Several causes were tossed about. Possibly the steel of the bridge had crystallized leading to the collapse of the north section of the bridge. Could the sandstone foundation which supported the bridge have settled? Maybe the lifting mechanism was tampered with or somehow damaged.

The two soldiers who were stationed on the bridge, Privates Adseh and Bellinger were interviewed. A key to the cause of the collapse became clear when the two soldiers stated that they did not hear the distinctive "click"of the bridge section locking into place when it lowered.

After a thorough search of the bridge, the investigators concluded that the bridge had not settled in a fully closed position and collapsed under the weight of the locomotive. It was a mechanical malfunction that caused the collapse of the bridge.

The result of the accident was the railroad engine, the tender and the wreckage from the north section of the bridge blocking the channel leading to the Davis and Poe locks. They were the only locks with a depth of 24-feet which permitted deep draft ships to lock through. The movement of iron ore was reduced, but in days the wreckage was removed and the two deep water locks were reopened.

Unfortunately, the train's conductor and engineer, David Monroe and H. J. Willis were not so lucky. They rode the engine to the bottom of the canal and were not able to free themselves from the wreckage. Their bodies were recovered from the engine.

# THE SURPRISE OF THE BIRD OF MICHIGAN CITY

**T**he packet freighter *India* was forced into the harbor seeking shelter from the storm raging on Lake Huron. As the *India* eased its way to the pier, 18 year old August Maxwell jumped from the deck of the ship onto the concrete breakwall pier to tie up the vessel. He lost his footing, slipped and fell backwards into the harbor.

The crew of the *India* and crews from other ships forced into the harbor by the storm made several attempts to rescue the man. Yawls were lowered and men even dove into the harbor to look for the young man, but it looked as though Lake Huron had claimed another sailor. The keeper on duty at the lighthouse who was watching the rescue attempts put in a call to the Coast Guard for assistance.

Captain Davidson and the crew of the Harbor Beach Coast Guard Station responded to the call in their motorized lifeboat. The Guardsmen maneuvered around the ships tied to the wall, looking under the turn of their hulls, and between the ships and the breakwall.

Captain Davidson boarded the *India* to gather information and direct the rescue activities. While on board he noticed a fishing tug, the *Bird of Michigan City*, moored near the *India*. The tug was sitting very low in the water; as if

----Bird of Michigan

*Ships sheltering at the Government harbor of refuge at Harbor Beach, Michigan. From the Tony Lang Collection.*

it were taking on water and about to settle to the bottom. A wood boat subjected to a Lake Huron storm could easily spring a seam below the waterline and take on water.

After the Guardsmen found the lifeless body of August Maxwell, they turned their attention towards the sinking fishing tug.

Captain Davidson, out of concern for the welfare of the crew aboard the ship, decided to board the *Bird of Michigan City*. Possibly the crew was exhausted from fighting the lake all day and turned in early, maybe they were unaware that their boat was taking on water.

Captain Davidson and one of his men boarded the fishing tug. A search of the craft revealed only one person, the engineer, asleep below. Knowing that fishing tugs usually carried more than a crew of one they wondered where the rest of the crew was.

Upon further investigation, they found the vessel wasn't sinking, rather it was found that the *Bird of Michigan City* was loaded down with a heavy cargo. The fishing tug was so packed that it weighed down the vessel.

The cargo was Canadian beer, $24,000 worth of "illegal" beer! She was packed so full it was said that another case wouldn't fit.

This was during the time of Prohibition. The 19th Amendment prohibited the sale and consumption of any alcoholic libation in the United States.

It was determined that the other crewmembers had left the craft undetected, when they saw the Coast Guard at the breakwall looking for the missing sailor.

The Coast Guard moved the *Bird of Michigan City* from the breakwall to the city dock to await the arrival of the prohibition officers from Detroit the following day. Under the close supervision of the City Police, Coast Guard and the Prohibition Officers, the cargo from the fishing tug was off loaded onto the dock. The spectacle of a huge pile of contraband drew a large crowd. The ship contained over 1000 cases of Canadian beer and ale!

The cases were loaded onto trucks and taken to the beach. There they were doused with oil and set afire. Any bottles which did not break in the fire were broken by the Prohibition Officers supervising the destruction of the evidence.

The crowd that gathered at the beach to witness the destruction of the illegal cargo rivaled the crowds that gathered at the Fourth of July celebration. Some of the onlookers cheered the capture of the illegal cargo while many others mourned the loss.

It was said that over 1000 cases were taken off the fishing tug, but there were far less than that burned on the beach. Mysteriously some of the illegal cargo disappeared from the trucks somewhere between the dock and the beach.

The *Bird of Michigan City* was the sinking vessel that wasn't sinking but the boat did create a lot of attention.

# THE MANASOO CAPSIZED IN THE STORM

**I**n the late 1800's, travel by lake ship was the most common method of transportation in the Great Lakes region. To meet the demand for transportation along the Canadian shore of Lake Ontario, the 154-foot *Macassa* was built at Glasgow, Scotland, brought to the Lakes and put into service in 1889.

The Hamilton Steamship Company of Hamilton, Ontario, had purchased the vessel to make a morning trip from Hamilton to Toronto and a return trip in the afternoon. The ship could carry 200 passengers and assorted freight. The ship was not designed for overnight travel so it did not have passenger cabins. Rather, the passengers were entertained while en route in various salons, dining halls, and bars.

The enterprise proved to be a success. There was plenty of cargo and passengers to make the trip. The Hamilton Steamship Company purchased another ship, the *Modjeska*, to join the *Macassa*. In addition a rival company put a ship, the *Turbinia*, on the run.

In 1905, with the increasing amount of cargo and passengers transported each year, the Hamilton Steamship Company decided to maximize the amount of cargo and passengers the

--Manasoo

**167**

*Macassa* could carry by increasing the size of the ship by 24-feet to 178-feet.

The three ships were very profitable for a time but automobile, truck and railroad traffic were eating into their volume of business. By 1927 the Turbinia was sold to operate elsewhere on the lake, and the *Macassa* was sold to the Owen Sound Transportation Company.

During the winter of 1927/1928, the Owen Sound Transportation Company renamed the *Macassa* to *Manasoo* and cabins were constructed on the ship providing passenger sleeping accommodations. Its new route required passenger sleeping quarters.

In 1928, her first season with the Owen Sound Transportation Company, the *Manasoo* transported passengers and cargo between Owen Sound, Ontario, Sault Ste. Marie, and Mackinaw Island. The owners of the company were looking forward to the 1929 season when they laid her up for the winter in early September.

Cattlemen from Oil Springs, Ontario kept a herd of cattle grazing on Manitoulin Island, but they needed to transport the cattle to the mainland before winter set in. The owners of the Owen Sound Transportation Company agreed to take the *Manasoo* out of winter lay-up and transport the cattle.

On September 14, 1928 the *Manasoo*, departed Owen Sound for Manitowaning on Manitoulin Island, a trip which would cover about 120 miles.

The trip to the island was uneventful since the crew was familiar with the course having regularly sailed it during the summer. Onboard were Captain John McKay, first mate Osborn Long, chief engineer Tom McCutcheon, the second mate, purser, first and second chef, waiter, wheelsmen, second engineer, oiler, watchmen, firemen, and deckhands, a crew of 21. Almost the entire crew was made up of men from Owen Sound and the surrounding area.

The 116 cattle were loaded, 47 aft and another 69 head forward in pens constructed in the cargo compartment. The cattle were separated in pens constructed across the ship, from the port to the starboard sides. They could move from one side of the ship to the other but not forward and aft.

Also aboard for that last sail of the season were two passengers, cattle drovers sent along to accompany the herd.

Once loaded, the ship departed Manitowaning and sailed northeast through Manitowaning Bay and passed through the narrow channel between Centre Island and the north coast of Manitoulin Island. After

168

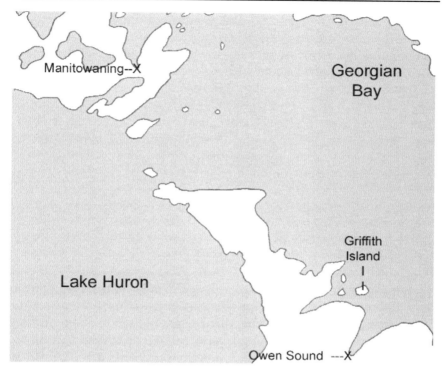

passing Cape Smith, Captain McKay could pick up the light at Lonely Island and use it to navigate across the open water of Georgian Bay. Then they would steam along the coast of the Bruce Peninsula to Griffith Island where the *Manasoo* would change its course to the south into the Owen Sound.

When the *Manasoo* rounded Cape Smith, Captain McKay found Georgian Bay being whipped up by a west wind. The Bay was rough and the wind was increasing, conditions which were not unusual on Georgian Bay in the fall.

Sailing in the lee of the Bruce Peninsula offered some protection from the ever increasing west wind and developing waves, but the *Manasoo* was riding nearly in the trough of the sea and rolling heavily. At about 3:00 am, the *Manasoo* had reached Griffith Island where she would begin a southern course. At that time of night most of the crew and the passengers were asleep.

Captain McKay called for a change of course to round Griffith Island. The wheelsman told the captain that she was not responding to the wheel as it should. The *Manasoo* was sluggish and getting hard to control.

The captain knew right away that there was a problem. When a ship was slow to respond to the wheel and sluggish it usually meant there was a problem with the rudder or that the vessel was taking on water. The captain sent the first mate below to assess the condition.

Captain McKay ordered the *Manasoo* towards the shallow water around Griffith Island. Fearing that the ship was sinking, beaching the ship was a far better option than sinking in deep water. However, before much progress was made towards the shallows, water had crept into the engine room and put out the boiler fire. The ship was now filling with lake water and without propulsion or pumps. The *Manasoo* was doomed!

Orders were given to lower the lifeboats. One was released but before any others could be lowered, without any prior indication, the *Manasoo* quickly rolled on her side.

The 40-year-old ship then slowly raised her bow as the stern sunk below surface. In minutes the ship slipped below the surface.

At three o'clock in the morning most of the crew was asleep down below in the crew quarters. Many of them were trapped in their bunks and drowned. Yet amazingly some people made it out of the ship.

The ship's purser, Art Middleboro, was in his cabin preparing for bed when he was thrown against the bulkhead when the ship rolled. He had the forethought to grab his life preserver and dressed only in his underwear he ran from his cabin and dove for the water just before the *Manasoo* sank.

Below decks, oiler Roy Fox, was in the engine room. As the ship rolled and started its downward plunge to the bottom, somehow Roy found his way out and swam frantically against the suction of the sinking ship to the surface.

The ship's raft was floating nearby and Roy swam towards it. The raft, which apparently had floated free when the ship sank, became the salvation of several men. Joining Roy Fox on the raft were Captain McKay, Chief Engineer McCutcheon, First Mate Long, the Purser and one of the cattle drovers, Mr. Wallace.

The storm, with gale force winds, churned the waters of the bay with waves that threatened to capsize the raft on each crest. The men on the raft watched as the lone lifeboat floated nearby. It was overturned but two men clung to it. The men on the raft could do nothing to help the men hanging onto the lifeboat but yell over the howling wind words of encouragement. The six men on the raft looked on in horror as the men clinging to the lifeboat were washed off into the Bay. The lifeboat was quickly blown out of sight.

# THE MANASOO CAPSIZED IN THE STORM

The strong west wind blew the raft away from Griffith Island, the closest land, into the open water of Georgian Bay, driven eastward by the 70 mile per hour winds into the bay. They knew their chances of being found were low, for where they were being blown few ships traveled, especially during a severe storm. About an hour after the *Manasoo* went down, the men grew excited when they saw the lights of a down-bound ship near them. Unfortunately, the ship didn't see them and it passed by in the storm. Another ship, this one up-bound, also passed by without sighting the men in the raft.

The six men huddled in the raft were benumbed by the cold wind and spray biting their flesh. The chief engineer seemed to be less able to withstand the horrendous conditions the men had to endure and succumbed to exposure.

The raft was not very stable in the breaking waves and each passing wave threatened to capsize it. The men had determined to push the engineer's body off the raft. The raft was sitting low and taking on water; the men hoped that the weight of one less man onboard would help to keep the raft afloat. Before the engineer was given up to Lake Huron he was stripped of his clothes. The purser had left the ship dressed only in his underwear and the clothes would now better serve the purser than the engineer.

By Monday afternoon the men had been driven before the wind for almost sixty hours. The men on the raft endured tremendous hardship. The constant movement of the raft formed painful blisters on the men and wind driven spray stung their reddened faces. Huge waves generated by the wind, tossed the raft about, threatening to capsize and send the weary sailors into the angry lake. They all knew if the raft capsized they wouldn't have the strength to climb back in. It would be the end for them.

The raft was blown about 15 miles east of Griffith Island where the *Manasoo* had sunk. They had just about given up hope when the steamer *S.S. Manitoba* sailed into view. The five survivors of the *Manasoo* on the raft were taken onboard and transported to Owen Sound, where they found out that they alone had lived through the sinking of the ship. Fourteen of their shipmates and one passenger had been claimed by the lake when the *Manasoo* sunk.

Captain McKay, from his hospital bed, theorized that the *Manasoo* must have sprung a seam aft, because the ship had first settled from the stern. Then in its unstable condition the ship quickly capsized. Had the *Manasoo* not capsized she might have made it to the shallows where all passengers and crew could have been saved.

The generally accepted cause of the *Manasoo* rolling… the cargo had shifted…the cattle panicked on the ship being tossed about in a storm and taking on water and gathered together on one side of the ship, causing the *Manasoo* to quickly roll over killing sixteen men and 116 head of cattle.

# THE GOLIATH IS ON FIRE!

**I**t was necessary for sailors on early steamships to keep a constant watch out for fire. The ships burned wood or coal in their firebox for steam and sparks from their smokestacks were often a source for many a ship fire. The steamer *Goliath* was the victim of just such a fire.

On September 13, 1848, the steamship *Goliath* fought her way up the St. Clair River Rapids at Port Huron, Michigan into the open waters of Lake Huron.

The ship had a full hold of cargo to deliver to the Lake Superior Mining Company. The *Goliath*, unlike most ships of her time, did not have paddlewheels for propulsion, rather the *Goliath* was one of the first steamships on the lakes to use propellers.

The propellers were not the three, four or five blades we are now familiar with. The two propellers on the *Goliath* were the newly patented "Ericsson's Screw Propeller." The Ericsson's Screw Propeller had a central core and an outer rim. The blades were attached between the core and outer rim.

Just completing her second season on the lakes, the *Goliath* was 131-feet in length, 26-feet in beam with a draft of 9-feet. The ship had been built at the city of St. Clair, Michigan.

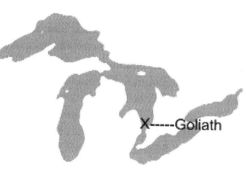

X-----Goliath

Several hours into the trip, the *Goliath* had covered about 45 miles up Lake Huron to about the village of White Rock. The village was so named for a large white rock just off shore. The rock was a gathering place for Native Americans that frequented the area and the pioneer families attracted by the vast forests.

On that mid September day, there was a brisk wind blowing in from the southeast by east. The people on shore looked out on the lake to see a ship about eight miles out with smoke bellowing from her. Smoke from a steamship isn't unusual but the amount of smoke coming from the steamer on the lake that day was unusual. It was obvious to those on shore that the ship was on fire.

The *Goliath* had caught on fire. No one knows for sure how the fire started, none of the 18 aboard lived to tell.

The fire might have started in the engine room where embers from the firebox landed on the oil soaked floor and often started small fires. Just for that reason, buckets of water were kept filled and within easy reach throughout the engine room.

The fire could also have started from errant sparks from the smokestack, a common problem with early steamships. The sparks would fall on the top of the wood cabin work covered with flammable paint and ignite. A constant watch was kept to extinguish the sparks before they became a bigger problem.

The steamer burned as the men looked on from shore. There was no signal from the vessel, no distress flag flying, but it was obvious to the men on shore that the occupants of the ship were in trouble.

Mr. Whitcomb, a farmer in the area, and some men attempted to launch a small boat to row to the aid of the crew of the burning ship but the waves breaking at the rocky shore prevented them from getting the boat out beyond the breakers. There was nothing anyone on shore could do.

The crew of the burning steamer could have taken to the lifeboat and escaped but they were probably fighting the fire hoping to save the ship.

One can only imagine the horror the crew experienced as they fought the fire aboard their boat as the ship continued to steam north. The *Goliath*, with flames destroying her deck work, covered another 10 miles north before she was destroyed.

The *Goliath* carried eighteen men, and a cargo of 20,000 bricks, 30,000 board feet of lumber, 40 tons of hay, and about 2,000 barrels of corn meal, flower, and other provisions. But there were another 200 barrels in the *Goliath's* cargo hold which spelled the end of the two-year-old ship. The ship also carried 200 kegs of black powder!

One can only guess that the crew was frantically fighting the fire to prevent it from reaching the explosive black powder. But when the fire reached the kegs, the *Goliath* exploded with such a fury that the explosion was heard sixty miles in any direction.

Charred remains of the *Goliath* washed up across Lake Huron on the Canadian shore, but no bodies of the eighteen member crew were ever found.

A fire onboard a ship is frightening. It's not like a house fire where hopefully one can leave the building. When fire strikes a boat there are two choices for a crew; stay and fight the fire or get off the ship. To stay and fight fortunately there is a never ending supply of water. When all attempts at putting out a fire are gone, hopefully there is a lifeboat or yawl available. But when the ship is carrying hundreds of kegs of highly explosive material, extinguishing a shipboard fire takes on added urgency to stay and fight; a fight the crew of the *Goliath* did not win.

# PARTY AT THE WILLIAM C. WARREN

**I**n February 1948, a drunken party was held on a beach on Lake Huron. The estimated three thousand merry makers gathered at Black Point, northwest of the Presque Isle lighthouse. The location was the site where the Canadian steamer *William C. Warren* had grounded in shallow water two months earlier.

Neal Curtis, a local Conservation Officer who observed the intoxicated bunch said, "It is the worst case of… intoxication he had ever witnessed." They came for the free meal that was said to be there but many became so inebriated the party goers staggered around the beach and interfered with the men who were attempting to salvage the cargo of the *Warren*.

The *William C. Warren*, a 400-foot Canadian grain carrier, was southbound on the lake during a horrendous blow. The ship, loaded with 80,000 bushels of wheat, struggled against the gale force winds and mounting seas. Captain MacBeth set a course for North Bay about 20 miles north of Alpena and about 18 miles east southeast of Rogers City. The bay would offer a refuge from the ravages of the stormy lake. Unfortunately, the course took them dangerously close to the rocky shoals of Black Point.

X--William C. Warren

*The* William C. Warren *ashore after the storm. The photo shows a crew member being transported on the breeches buoy. From the William D. Lewis Collection.*

The *William C. Warren* ground to a halt in the shoal water of Black Point riding up high on the rocky bottom. The waves crashed over the stranded steamer and washed the decks with torrents of water.

When attempts of the *Warren* to free herself from the rocks failed, the captain made a call to the Great Lakes Towing Company in Sarnia, Ontario, for assistance. The wrecking tug *Favorite* and a barge were brought alongside the crippled steamer and some cargo was removed to lighten the vessel but when the *Warren's* engines roared and belched black smoke into the cold November sky the ship still would not budge. Finally a line was run from the tug *Favorite*. The tug drew up the slack from the line and the captain called for full power as the tug churned up the water into a white foam. Again the *Warren* did

*The* William C. Warren *aground and frozen in place in North Bay. The photograph shows work being done to salvage her cargo. From the William D. Lewis Collection.*

not move. Further attempts by the tug were not successful and the Canadian steamer remained on the rocks.

After it was found that the ship probably could not be removed from the rocky bottom, the owners of the *Warren*, Upton-St. Lawrence Transportation Company, and its insurance underwriter determined the ship to be a total loss. The insurance underwriter paid out to the owners of the ship, and the hulk remained on the rocks.

Tom Reid, owner of the Great Lakes Towing Company, purchased the rights to salvage the *William C. Warren* from the insurance underwriters for the sum of $5,000. With his expertise he was sure the ship could be removed from its resting place. In April of 1948 he returned to Black Point and worked to free the *Warren* from the rocky bottom. With much effort the *Warren* was removed from the shoal water and the leaking, crippled vessel was towed to a dry dock in Collingwood, Ontario.

The ship was repaired and put back into service. Since then, the *William C. Warren* has earned well over its estimated value of a half of a million dollars. The $5,000 was an excellent investment on the part of Tom Reid.

Prior to the *Warren* being removed from the rocks of Black Point, the cargo was sold to two local men, Alfred Erkfitz of Rogers City and Moore Combs of Hillman. They rigged a pipeline from shore 800-feet out into the lake to the ill-fated ship. The cargo of wheat was then pumped to shore. But, the salvage attempt was fraught with problems. An early winter caused ice to form at the wreck site, hampering their efforts. If the wind blew in from the south it would take the ice out, but when the wind came from the north the ice would blow back in. In addition to the weather inhibiting the salvage work, the drunks staggered around the workers, getting in their way and slowed progress. The workmen were not involved in the public display of alcoholism but it did hinder their work on the cargo recovery.

The free meal lured them in, many ate and some became so drunk they couldn't... fly. The drunks at the site of the wrecked steamer *William C. Warren* were... ducks. They ate the wheat cargo which had become wet and fermented in the cargo holds.

Neal Curtis, a local conservation officer said. "It's the worst case of wildlife intoxication he has ever witnessed. They would get so drunk they would just flop and stagger around."

# THE STORM OF NOVEMBER 1966

The Great Lakes give Michigan's lower and upper peninsulas their unique shape. Lakes Michigan and Huron provide the lower peninsula its east and west coasts. Lake Michigan forms the south coast of the Upper Peninsula and Lake Superior the north shore.

These vast expanses of water provide fresh water to the towns and cities surrounding the lakes. It also serves as a highway to transport the areas mineral riches, and they are a recreational boater's dream. But the lakes also influence Michigan's weather.

The weather systems sweep into the Midwest from almost any direction and cross the Great Lakes before they strike the Upper or Lower Peninsula, or both.

A storm passing over the lakes picks up moisture only to drop it on the mainland of Michigan as rain or snow. The winds race across the lakes unimpeded, sometimes building into hurricane force blows. The winds also create huge waves not uncommonly reaching the height of two or three story buildings.

The storm of November 29, 1966 roared down from the north dumping up to 15 inches of snow on the Upper Peninsula. Snow

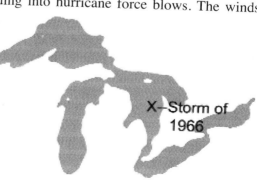

X–Storm of 1966

# STRANGE & UNUSUAL SHIPWRECKS ON THE GREAT LAKES

*The 729-foot* Edmund Fitzgerald *reported being battered by the storm as it ran the length of Lake Superior. From the photographic collection of the Bayliss Public Library.*

blown by 70 mile per hour wind gusts created 7-foot snowdrifts. At least 600 students from Michigan Technological University and Northern Michigan University returning from Thanksgiving break abandoned their snowbound cars and buses to seek shelter.

Twenty to 30-foot waves and hurricane force winds raised havoc on all of the Great Lakes. The *Chesapeake* and Ohio ferry, *City of Midland 41*, while entering Ludington Harbor, was blown onto a sandy reef. The 128 passengers remained on the 470-foot ship and whiled away the time playing cards and eating sumptuous meals. When the storm subsided, they were taken off the ship safely. Captain Peter Pulcer of the Columbia Transportation Company's *Edmund Fitzgerald*, reported that he had battled a storm all of the way across Lake Superior.

During the storm there were a lot of ships out on Lake Huron. The 451-foot freighter *Howard L. Shaw* was heading north on Lake Huron barely able to make one mile per hour through the wind and waves. The wheelsman struggled at the wheel to keep the ship's bow into the wind. He swung the wheel fully from port to starboard trying to maintain control when suddenly the *Shaw* was blown around until it was heading south! The *Howard L. Shaw* tried twice to come about and regain its

**182**

*The 586-foot steamer* Robert Hobson. *From the Hugh Clark Great Lakes Photographic Collection.*

course, but both attempts failed so they continued on south seeking shelter at Sarnia, Ontario.

The 586-foot *S.S. Robert Hobson* was 4 miles north of the Harbor Beach light when it was blown around and elected to continue south and return to the St. Clair River

A few days earlier, on November 21, 1966, the 470-foot West German Freighter *Nordmeer* abruptly grounded on a shoal near Alpena, Michigan. The weather was clear with little wind. The shoal was marked with a lighted buoy which flashed green every four seconds, but through pilot error the ship had run hard aground on Thunder Bay Island Shoal.

Within minutes the engine room and cargo holds, filled with 990 coils of steel bound for Chicago, began to fill from the breech in her hull. An S.O.S. was sent from the ship and the first to respond was the Canadian freighter *Samuel Mather*. The *Mather* took off thirty-five of the 43 sailors aboard the German Freighter. Remaining onboard were the captain and seven others to protect the salvage rights of the cargo and ship.

*The steamer* Samuel Mather *passing through the St. Clair River at Port Huron. From the Hugh Clark Great Lakes Photographic Collection.*

When the weather blew in five days later, on November 26, the *Nordmeer* was beaten by the relentless waves. Each wave ground the ship onto the rocky shoal, breaking the keel of the freighter and ripping out its bottom. The captain, fearing for the lives of his skeletal crew, sent out an S.O.S. The eight men wanted off the stricken freighter. They had two motorized lifeboats at their disposal, but the conditions were too terrible to launch.

The Coast Guard Cutter *Mackinaw* left its homeport at once but it was still several hours away. A Coast Guard helicopter took off towards the grounded ship but the conditions wouldn't allow it to pick the men off the *Nordmeer*. Fortunately, there was a lull in the storm just long enough for the helicopter to lift the men to safety.

The 592-foot *S.S. Kinsman Independent,* loaded with coal, passed through the St. Clair River into southern Lake Huron. Captain Newman reported that the winds were light and from the west. Sixty miles north while off the Harbor Beach Light, the conditions had changed. The winds were coming from the north at 50 to 60 miles per hour. The *Kinsman Independent* was blown off course and wallowed in the trough of the waves for a few fearful minutes before it was able to reverse its course and return to the safety of Port Huron.

Not all freighters turned around in the storm. The *Edward Y. Townsend* and its sister ship in the Bethlehem Fleet, the *Daniel J. Morrell* passed up through the river into Lake Huron.

Both ships, in their 60th season on the Lakes, were traveling in ballast having unloaded their cargo of Taconite pellets at the Bethlehem Steel Plant at Buffalo, New York. The 603-foot *Morrell* anchored below Detroit due to the storm. The 602-foot *Townsend* passed her sister and anchored below Stag Island in the St. Clair River. Both ships were bound for Taconite Harbor, Minnesota.

Captain Crawley, master of the *Morrell*, and Master of the *Townsend*, Captain Connelly, stayed in radio communication, discussing the storm and conditions in Lake Huron.

The *Daniel J. Morrell* heaved anchor and traveled up into Lake Huron. The *Townsend* followed several miles behind. The weather in lower Lake Huron at the time was light westerly winds.

Sixty miles into the trip up Lake Huron found the two ships off the Harbor Beach Light. At that time the wind was blowing at 35 miles per hour and increasing and the seas were 8-feet and mounting. The *Morrell* was several miles ahead of the *Townsend* but the snow blizzard prevented visual contact.

*The* Daniel J. Morrell. *From the State of Michigan Archives, Lansing, Michigan.*

The two captains discussed the possibility of turning back but they didn't want to chance turning around in the seas and winds, being light. If they carried a full cargo the additional weight would have made them more maneuverable for the conditions. They also talked about heading to Thunder Bay to shelter there.

The *Townsend* began to blow around, or broach into the sea. The ship fell off to starboard and left full rudder was required before the ship was brought back on course. When Captain Connelly reported the incident to Captain Crawley of the *Morrell*, Crawley said they had had a similar situation but all was well now.

The wind had increased to 65 miles per hour and the seas, which Captain Connelly described as "tremendous", were running at 20- to 25-feet. The *Townsend* reported she was pitching, rolling and pounding in the seas. Several times solid water was taken over the bow.

There were other ships out on Lake Huron that day trying to keep on course in the storm. The 615-foot *S.S. Harry Coulby* was about six miles north of Port Sanilac, Michigan when it took solid water over her bow from a 20-foot wave. The captain was informed via radio that conditions further north were much worse. He gave the orders to come about and set a course back to Port Huron.

The captain of the *S.S. Fred A. Manske* reported his ship was almost blown around but they were able to fight it. He said he was reluctant to come about in the seas because the self un-loading equipment made the

*The* Fred A. Manske *in calmer waters. From the Hugh Clark Great Lakes Photographic Collection.*

*Manske* top heavy. The ship made it through the dangerous Point Aux Barques area and arrived safely at its destination.

The *Edward Y. Townsend* battled its way through the storm and arrived at Sault Ste. Marie and found that her sister ship, the *Daniel J. Morrell* had not yet arrived. Captain Connelly promptly notified the Bethlehem Steel headquarters in Cleveland, Ohio that the *Morrell* was overdue. Amazingly, the company waited almost a full day before informing the Coast Guard of the missing *Daniel J. Morrell*.

Once told of the missing steamer, the Coast Guard sent out a notice to all mariners that the *Daniel J. Morrell* was overdue and asked all ships to keep an eye out for her. Sailing through a storm as vicious as this one, anything could have happened. A ship could have all of its electronics, including the radio disabled or the ship could be otherwise disabled and be sheltering in some desolate cove.

The mystery of the *Morrell* was further heightened when the *G.G. Post* recovered the body of a sailor in a lifejacket with the name *Morrell* stenciled on it. An empty life raft, life ring and several more bodies from the *Morrell* were found and everyone knew the *Daniel J. Morrell* had met with disaster during the storm that ravaged the Great Lakes that November day in 1966.

It wasn't until 38 hours after the ship had sunk that the story surrounding the sinking of the *Daniel J. Morrell* came to light. That is when the forward life raft with 4 men from the *Morrell* was found.

Onboard the raft were Art Stojek, John Cleary, Charles Fosbender and Dennis Hale. All had succumbed to the elements except Dennis Hale.

Deck watchman Hale, from his bed at Harbor Beach Hospital, suffering from exposure, told of the demise of the freighter *Daniel J. Morrell*.

Hale had gone to his quarters after getting off his watch. At about 2:00 am Hale was awakened by two loud bangs. He turned on his cabin light but it didn't work, then the alarm sounded. He grabbed his lifejacket and made way through the darkness to the deck. As he looked back he could see lights glowing in the stern of the ship. He also noticed the ship was hog-backed (raised in the center) an indication that the keel of the ship had been damaged.

Dennis Hale returned to his quarters to get dressed, but in the dark he couldn't find his pants, only his peacoat. At the forward life raft Dennis, dressed only in a peacoat, boxer shorts and a lifejacket, met several other crewmen. They all sat in the life raft and awaited the ship to sink allowing the raft to float free.

Hale described seeing the deck in the vicinity of hatches 11 and 12 begin being ripped apart from the starboard side to port. Through the action of the wind and waves, the stern section rose high on a wave crest while the bow was low in a trough. The motion broke the ship in half.

The stern section, still under power, rammed the forward section several times, pushing it aside to port. Hale reported that the stern powered by and off into the distance.

The 603-foot long mighty *Daniel J. Morrell*, once the largest ship to sail on the Great Lakes, had broken in two! The bow quickly sank and the stern powered some 5 miles away before it sank.

Twenty eight men met their deaths that day on Lake Huron, only Dennis Hale miraculously living through the ordeal.

Captain Connelly, Master of the *Townsend*, conducted a heavy weather damage survey of his ship. He was concerned for his ship after battling through the tremendous storm that assaulted Lake Huron and had broken and sunk the *Daniel J. Morrell*. A crack was found on one of the deck plates.

A one eighth inch wide by eighteen inch long crack on the deck was found extending from the combing of the hatch cover towards the center of the ship.

Almost immediately, the Marine Inspection Bureau pulled the sailing certificate of the *Edward Y. Townsend*. They deemed the ship un-seaworthy. Without a certificate, the ship could not be used to carry cargo or crew until it was repaired.

Ironically, the *Edward Y. Townsend*, the sister ship to the *Daniel J. Morrell*, was found to be un-seaworthy and too expensive to repair. Like her sister, her career was over.

The *Townsend* was sold to a foreign company for scrap. It was to be towed through the lakes and across the Atlantic Ocean where it would be torn apart, piece by piece and melted down.

But, while in tow across the Atlantic, the tow boat and the *Townsend* encountered rough weather. In the storm the *Townsend*, like her sister ship the *Daniel J. Morrell*, broke her keel and sank to the bottom.

*(Note: For an excellent description of the sinking of the* Daniel J. Morrell *and Dennis Hale's battle to survive through his 38 hours on a life raft, read the book,* Sole Survivor: Dennis Hale's Own Story. *Lakeshore Charters & Marine Exploration, Inc. Lexington, Michigan. 1996)*

# GLOSSARY

**Abandon Ship Signal** - A long blast on the ship's whistle notifying everyone onboard that the ship is in severe peril and for all to leave the ship by lifeboats or any means immediately.

**Aft** - Towards the rear end of a ship.

**Beam** - The largest width of a ship.

**Barge** - A barge is designed or rebuilt as a vessel to be pushed or pulled by another ship. The barge, usually without any means of propulsion, transports cargo on the Great Lakes and its harbors and tributaries.

**Bilge** - Lowest part of the interior of a ship's hull.

**Bit** - A wood or metal structural post on a tugboat to which the towline is attached.

**Boiler** - A metal container where water is heated to create steam to power the steam engines.

**Bollard** - A post or cast metal device on a dock or wharf. The mooring lines of a ship are secured to it to hold the ship to the dock or wharf.

**Bow** - The front end of a ship. The port bow, starboard bow refers to the left and right of the forward sides of the vessel.

**Breakers** - The waves crashing on the shore or rocks.

**Bridge** - The pilothouse or wheelhouse. The location on the ship where the ship is steered.

**Capsize** - When a ship turns over; rolls over to the port or starboard.

**Checking Speed** - To reduce speed.

**Chief Engineer** - The crew member who is in charge of the engine and machinery of the ship.

**Companionway, Passageway** - A passage, corridor, or hallway on a ship.

**Davits** - The brackets which hold lifeboats on the ship and are used to raise or lower the lifeboats.

**Deadlights** - Portholes.

**Deck Cargo** - Cargo transported on the deck of a ship rather than in the hold below deck.

**Distress Signal** - A signal used to alert others of a disaster at sea and call for assistance.

**Drydock** - An area where a ship sails in and the water is pumped out. The drydock allows repairs to be made to the hull below the water line.

**Firebox** - The chamber in which a fire is built to heat the water in the boiler on a steam powered ship.

**First Mate** - Second in command of the ship behind the captain. To be a mate the person must meet federal licensing requirements.

**Fog Signal** - A steam or compressed air powered whistle sounded in times of reduced visibility to notify other ships.

**Fore** - The forward or front of the ship.

**Foredeck** - A deck towards the bow of a ship.

**Founder** - To sink.

**Freeboard** - The part of a ship's hull above the surface of the water.

**Freshening** - The wind increasing; the wind is freshening.

**Full Ahead** - A ship moving at top speed in a forward direction.

**Gale Force Wind** - A strong wind from 32 to 63 miles per hour.

**Gangway** - A passageway in a side of a ship where passengers and cargo enter and depart the vessel.

**Glass or Glasses** - A telescope or binoculars.

**Harbor of Refuge** - A harbor, natural or man made, designed for ships to seek refuge in times of severe weather.

**Hawser** - A large rope used to tow or secure a ship.

**Hold** - An area on a ship below the deck where cargo is stowed.

**Holed** - A hull of a ship being punctured in a collision or by striking an object.

**Hull** - The body of the vessel.

**Jacob's Ladder** - A rope ladder.

**Keel** - A large wood or steel beam running bow to stern at the lowest point of the ship. It forms the backbone of the ship.

**Knot** - Speed of a ship which equals one nautical mile per hour.

**Lee** - Protection; the side of a ship protected from the wind.

**Lifeboat Station** - The location of a lifeboat on a ship.

**Life Jackets, Life Preserver** - a personal floatation device used to support an individual at the surface of the water.

**Lightened** - Intentionally reducing the weight of the ship.

**Lines** - Ropes used on a ship.

**List** - When a ship leans to port or starboard, left or right, due to unevenly stored cargo or from taking on water.

**Lumber Hooker** - A ship involved with the transportation of wood products.

**Mid Ship** - In the middle of the ship from the bow to the stern.

**Mooring Lines** - Lines used to secure a vessel to a dock, pier or wharf.

**Passenger Ship** - A ship designed to transport passengers on journeys extending more than just a few hours.

**Range Lights** - Lighted beacons spaced a distance from one another. A ship is on course when entering a river or harbor when it positions itself so the lights are aligned above one another.

**Pilothouse** - The bridge of a ship; where the ship is controlled, steered, and navigated.

**Pitch** - The forward and aft rocking of a ship.

# GLOSSARY

**Port** - The left side of a boat when looking towards the front.

**Prow** - The forward part of a vessel.

**Radar** - A device which sends out a strong beam of radio waves. When it strikes an object it reflects back. The radar can then determine the distance away, direction of movement and speed of the object.

**Reef** - A rocky or sandy feature at or near the surface of the water.

**Roll** - The sideward, port to starboard, movement of a ship.

**Schooner** - A sailing craft having two masts, one fore, the other aft.

**Shipping Lane** - Areas of a lake which ships must be traveling in a specific direction; up bound or down bound lanes.

**Shoal Water** - Shallow water.

**Slow Astern** - A ship operating at slow speed in a backward direction.

**Soo Locks** - Situated between Lakes Superior and Huron the locks raise ships 22-feet to the higher level of Lake Superior, or lower downbound ships to the Lake Huron level.

**Starboard** - The right side of a boat when looking towards the bow.

**Stern** - The aft or rear of a boat.

**Swing Bridge** - A bridge which rotates from a central position. The bridge remains open for ship traffic to pass and closes only when it is needed. It is usually used for railroad bridges.

**Tanker** - A vessel specifically designed to transport liquid cargo, such as gasoline or other forms of oil.

**Telegraph** - A mechanical devise used to transmit instructions to and from the bridge of a ship to the engine room.

**Tender** - A small boat which carries crew, passengers and supplies between a ship or lighthouse and shore.

**Tug** - The workhorse of the lakes. Tugs have been used to assist other ships to docks, or through congested waterways, tow barges, to transport cargo and passengers, for fishing, ice breaking, as a wrecking vessel and as a rescue vessel.

**Turned Turtle** - A common phrase to describe a ship which has been capsized and its bottom is above the surface.

**Wharf** - A structure built along a waterway where ships can tie up and discharge or take on cargo or passengers.

**Wheelsman** - The person who met the licensing restriction to be qualified to steer the ship.

**Yawl** - A small boat on a ship used by the crew to get to shore from an anchorage.

# BIBLIOGRAPHY

## THE STORM OF SEPTEMBER 1930
*Grand Valley Daily Tribune*, Grand Haven, Michigan, September 27, 28, October 8, 1930.

*Ludington Daily News*, Ludington, Michigan, September 29, 1930.

*Ludington Sunday Morning News*, Ludington, Michigan, September 28, 1930.

*Muskegon Chronicle*, Muskegon, Michigan, September 27, 28, 1930.

## A STRANGE ACCOUNT FROM THE STORM OF 1913
Deedler, William, R., "Hell Hath No Fury Like a Great Lakes Fall Storm; Great Lakes White Hurricane November 1913." http://www.crh.noaa.gov/dtx/stm_1913.html.

Doner, Mary Francis, "The Salvager, The life of Captain Tom Reid on the Great Lakes." Ross and Haines Inc., Minneapolis, Minnesota, 1958.

Historical Collection of the Great Lakes, Bowling Green State University.

Swayze, David D., *Shipwreck!*, Harbor House Publishers, Inc., Boyne City, Michigan, 1992.

## SHIPS AND BRIDGES; HOUGHTON/HANCOCK
Houghton Historical Society, Upper Peninsula Digitization Center Collection.

http://michiganhighways.org/indepth/zilwaukee.html. The Zilwaukee Bridge.

Michigan Department of Transportation. http://www.michigan.gov/mdot/0.1607,7151-9620_11154-11188-28585-,00.html.

The history of the three bridges to span the canal between Houghton and Hancock, Kevin E. Musser, the Copper Range Railroad and Copper Country Historical Homepage.

Swayze, David D., *Shipwreck!*, Harbor House Publishers, Inc., Boyne City, Michigan, 1992.

## THE FISHING TUG SEARCHLIGHT
Swayze, David D., *Shipwreck!*, Harbor House Publishers, Inc., Boyne City, Michigan, 1992.

*The Huron County Tribune*, April 26, 1907.

*The Harbor Beach Times*, April 25, 1907.

*The Harbor Beach Times*, May 2, 1907.

*The Harbor Beach Times*, May 9, 1907.

*The Port Huron Times-Herald*, November 12, 1913.

*The Daily Herald*, April 24, 1907.

*The Daily Herald*, April 25, 1907.

## THE JINX OF CAPTAIN WALTER NEAL
*The Bay Mills News*, *Bay Mills Indian Community*, Brimley, Michigan, Vol. 7 No. 25, November 6, 2003, "Treacherous Lake Superior sinks the *Myron* in 1919", From the Bay Mills History Department.

*The Evening News*, Sault Saint Marie, Michigan, May 14, 16, 17, 1921.

The *Myron*, http://home.eznet.net/~dminor/TM990619.html.

Swayze, David D., *Shipwreck!*, Harbor House Publishers, Inc., Boyne City, Michigan, 1992.

## THE CAPTAIN'S AUNT
Historical Collection of the Great Lakes, Bowling Green State University.

# BIBLIOGRAPHY

Mansfield, J. B., editor, *History of the Great Lakes*. Volume I, Chicago, Illinois, Beers & Company, 1899. Transcribed for the Maritime History of the Great Lakes site by Walter Lewis and Brendon Ballard, http://www.hhpl.on.ca/GreatLakes/Documents/HGI/defalt.asp?ID=s026.

*News Herald,* Conneaut, Ohio, "Lake Erie: A Graveyard for Sailors," Catherine Ellsworth, September 29, 1986.

Swayze, David D., *Shipwreck!*, Harbor House Publishers, Inc., Boyne City, Michigan, 1992.

## ACCIDENT AT THE SOO LOCKS

*Locks and Ships*, The Soo Locks Boat Tours, Sault Ste. Marie.

*The Evening News*, Sault Ste. Marie, Michigan June 9, 10, 11, 12, 14, 1909.

"The Soo Locks" http://www.geo.msu.edu/geo333/SooLock.html.

United States Army Corp of Engineers, Detroit District, Operations Technical Support. "The History of the Soo Locks", http://huron.Ire.usace.army.mil/SOO/lockhist.html.

## E.M. FORD SANK LIKE A ROCK

The Scanner, The Toronto Marine Historical Society http://www.hhpl.on.ca/GreatLakes/Documents/Scanner/07/08/defaults.as.

*E.M. Ford*, Presque Isle. By Brian Ferguson, http://www.boatnerd.com/pictures/fleet/emford.htm.

*Milwaukee Sentinel*, Milwaukee, Wisconsin, December 26, 1979.

*Inland Seas*, Volume 55, Number 2, 1999, *The* E.M. Ford, Patrick Lapinski.

Swayze, David D., *Shipwreck!*, Harbor House Publishers, Inc., Boyne City, Michigan, 1992.

*The Evening News*, Sault Saint Marie, Michigan, December 26, 1979.

*The Alpena News*, Alpena, Michigan, December 26, 27, 1979.

## THE SCHOONER WILLIAM R. HANNA SAILS BY THE HARBOR

*The Harbor Beach Times*, November 11, 1880.

Burley, Dale, *The Harbor Beach Catalog*, 1982, Harbor Beach, Michigan.

## GERMAN SUBMARINE IN THE GREAT LAKES!

The *Eastland* Disaster Society, http://www.eastlanddisaster.org/uc97.htm.

*Chicago Tribune*, Chicago, Illinois, January 28, 1998.

*Chicago Daily Tribune*, Chicago, Illinois, June 8, 1921.

*Chicago Sunday Tribune*, Chicago, Illinois, August 17, 1919.

Discovered by A&T Recovery in 1992. http://scubachicago.com/yes-a-sub.htm.

Navy History, *UC-97*, http://www.historycentral.com/Navy/Submarine/uc-97.html.

Submarine Wrecks on the Great Lakes, http://www.ship-wreck.com/mesages/415.html.

## THE HUNTER SAVIDGE VS. MOTHER NATURE

Point aux Barques Lighthouse Museum, Point aux Barques, Michigan.

*The Alpena Evening News*, August 21, 22, 23, 24, 26, 28, 1899.

*The Alpena Argus*, August 28, 29, 1899.

*The Bad Axe Weekly Republican*, August 22, 1899.

*The Great Lakes Mariners*, Vol. 1 No. 6, 2002.

*The Harbor Beach Times*, August 22, 1899.

*The Lakeshore Guardian*, July 2002.

*The Lakeshore Guardian*, June 2002.

*The Lakeshore Guardian*, May 2002.

The Point aux Barques Lighthouse Museum.

*The Port Huron Sunday Herald*, November 19, 1892.

*The Port Huron Sunday Herald*, August 21, 1899.

Swayze, David D., *Shipwreck!*, Harbor House Publishers, Inc., Boyne City, Michigan, 1992.

## THE STRANGE AND TRAGIC TALE OF THE S.S. EASTLAND

Bell System Memorial, http://www.bellsysyemmemorial.com/eastland.html.

Chicago Historical Information, http://www.chipublic.org/004chicago'disasters/east-land_photos.html.

*Eastland* Disaster Historical Society, http://eastlanddisaster.org.html.

Hilton, George, W., *Eastland* Legacy of the *Titanic*, Stanford, University Press, Stanford, California, 1995.

Historical Collection of the Great Lakes, Bowling Green State University.

Swayze, David D., *Shipwreck!*, Harbor House Publishers, Inc., Boyne City, Michigan, 1992.

*The Chicago Sunday Tribune*, July 25, 1915.

*The Daily News*, Lake Steamer capsizes in Chicago River, http://www.inficad.com/~ksup/pm_oct15.html.

The *Eastland*, http://www.rmstitanichistory.com/eastland.html.

The *Eastland* Disaster, http://chicago.about.com/library/blank/bleastland01.html.

The *Eastland* Disaster of 1915, http://www.novagate.net/~bonevelle/eastland/.

*The Huron County Independent*, July 30, 1915.

## THE WINDOC AND THE BRIDGE

http://www.boatnerd.com/windoc/ *Windoc* Accident August 11, 2001.

http:www.wellandcanal.ca/transit/2001/august/windocstory.html, *Windoc* & Bridge 11 collision – August 11, 2001.

http://www.wellandcanal.com/mishap.html *Windoc* hit by Allanburg lift-bridge.

Swayze, David D., *Shipwreck!*, Harbor House Publishers, Inc., Boyne City, Michigan, 1992.

*Telescope*, Great Lakes Maritime Institute, Detroit Michigan, November – December 2001.

Transportation Safety Board of Canada, *Marine Reflexions Magazine*, Issue 22, July 2005. http:www.tsb.gc.ca/en/publications/reflexions/marine/2005/issue_22.

## THE CHARLES H. BRADLEY LOSES IN THE END

*Copper Country Reflections*, Portage Lake and Lake Superior Ship Canal, http://www.pasty.com/reflections/id318.htm.

*Daily Mining Gazette*, Houghton, Michigan, October 10, 1931.

Exploring Houghton and Hancock in the Upper Peninsula of Michigan, http://www.exploringthenorth.com/houghton/main.html.

*Marquette Mining Journal*, Marquette, Michigan, October 10, 1931.

# BIBLIOGRAPHY

*The Alpena News*, Alpena, Michigan, July 19, 20, 21, 1920.

## THE FIFTH TRIP OF THE WILLIAM C. MORELAND
Doner, Mary Francis, *The Salvager, The life of Captain Tom Reid On the Great Lakes*, Ross and Haines Inc., Minneapolis, Minnesota, 1958.

*Inland Seas*, Volume 5.2, 1949.

*Marquette Mining Journal*, Marquette Michigan, October 20, 21, 1910.

Swartz, David D., *Shipwreck!*, Harbor House Publications, Boyne City, Michigan, 1992.

The *W.C. Moreland*, http://filias.net/narcosis/sawtooth.htm.

*The Scanner*, Monthly News Bulletin of the Toronto Marine Historical Society, Ship of the month No. 4 *Parkdale*, http://www.hhpl.on.ca/GreatLakes/Documents/Scanner/02/03/default.asp?ID=c004, http://www.hhpl.on.ca/GreatLakes/Documents/Scanner/02/03/default.asp?ID=c007.

*William C. Moreland*, http://www.shipwrecks.net/shipwrecks/keweenaw/moreland.html.

## LOADING OF THE ANN ARBOR #4
Ann Arbor Railroad, http://www.annarbor-railroad.com/history.html.

Central Michigan University, Clark Historical Library, *Michigan's Ann Arbor Railroads; Rails to Water*, http://clarke.cmich.edu/michrailroads/water.htm.

Frederickson, Arthur and Lucy, *Frederickson's History of the Ann Arbor Auto and Train Ferries*, Gull Nest Publishing, Frankfort, Michigan, 1994.

*Manistique Pioneer-Tribune*, Manistique, Michigan, June 4, 11, 25, 1909.

Swayze, David D., *Shipwreck!*, Harbor House Publishers, Inc., Boyne City, Michigan, 1992.

*The Great Lakes Car Ferries*, Howell-North Books, Berkeley, California, 1962.

## KEEPER CAPTAIN KIAH AND HIS HEROIC SURFMEN
Swayze, David D., *Shipwreck!*, Harbor House Publishers, Inc., Boyne City, Michigan, 1992.

*The Huron County Tribune*, April 1880.

The Point Aux Barques Lighthouse Preservation Society.

Burley, Dale, The Harbor Beach Catalog, 1982, Harbor Beach, Michigan.

## THE LAST VOYAGE OF THE YACHT GUNILDA
Breining, Greg, *Wild Shore*, University of Minnesota Press, Minneapolis, 2000, http://www.gregbreining.com/excerpt1.html.

Chisholm, Barbara, *Superior: Under the shadow of the Gods: A guide to the history of the Canadian shore of Lake Superior*, Lynx Images Inc. Toronto, Canada, 2001.

TEKDIV Exploration, The *Gunilda* (Canada), http://www.tekdiv.com/the_gunilda.htm.

Historical Collection of the Great Lakes, Bowling Green State University.

Ertel, Darryl, and Matt Turchi, *Immersed, The* Gunilda, http://www.immersed.com/Articles/gunilda.htm.
195

# STRANGE & UNUSUAL SHIPWRECKS ON THE GREAT LAKES

## THE WHITE STAR IS BURNING!
Swayze, David D., *Shipwreck!*, Harbor House Publishers, Inc., Boyne City, Michigan, 1992.

*Port Huron Daily Times*, March 9, 1901.

## THE PASSENGER SHIP CHRISTOPHER COLUMBUS
*Christopher Columbus*, http://college.hmco/history/readerscomp/ships/html.

*Great Lakes Mariner*, Volume 3, Number 8, 2005.

Historical Collection of the Great Lakes, Bowling Green State University.

*Inland Seas*, "Harbor Disaster." By James R. Ward, Volume 16.2, 1960.

*Inland Seas*, "The *Christopher Columbus*." By Ernest H. Rankin, Volume 23.4, 1967.

*Inland Seas*, "The *Christopher Columbus*, a Favorite in Her Day." Volume 29.2, 1973.

*Inland Seas*, "Bicycling on the *Christopher Columbus*." By Richard F. Palmer, Volume 52.4, 1996.

Swayze, David D., *Shipwreck!*, Harbor House Publishers, Inc., Boyne City, Michigan, 1992.

## THE DISAPPEARANCE OF THE INKERMAN & CERISOLES
Barfknecht, Gary W., *Unexplained Michigan Mysteries*, Friede Publications, Davison, Michigan, 1993.

Chisholm, Barbara, *Superior: Under the shadow of the Gods: A guide to the history of the Canadian shore of Lake Superior*, Lynx Images Inc. Toronto, Canada, 2001.

*Duluth Herald*, Duluth, Minnesota, December 3, 5, 6, 7, 11, 16, 1918.

*Superior Shoals: The Underwater Mountain & Vanished Ships*, http://www.lynximages.com/shoal.htm.

Historical Collection of the Great Lakes, Bowling Green State University.

Swayze, David D., *Shipwreck!*, Harbor House Publishers, Inc., Boyne City, Michigan, 1992.

*The Sinking of the French Minesweepers* Inkerman *and* Cerisoles *in 1918*, Richard Ticknor, Thunder Bay Historical Museum Society, Papers and Records, Volume 1 1973.

Wildheart-Ventures, The Michipicoten Island Home Page, *Sailors' Bones*, David C. Whyte, http://www.wildheart-ventures.com/mich_home.html.

## THE SINKING OF THE TUG BLISH
*Detroit Free Press*, Detroit, Michigan, April 23, 1862.

Swayze, David D., *Shipwreck!*, Harbor House Publishers, Inc., Boyne City, Michigan, 1992.

## CAPTAIN MATTISON AND THE D.L. FILER
Historical Collections of Ohio, Diaries of S. J. Kelly, Plains Dealer, by Darlene E. Kelly.
http://www..rootsweb.com/~usgenweb/oh/newspapers/erie/part 5.txt
http://www..rootsweb.com/~usgenweb/oh/newspapers/erie/part 6.txt.

*The Detroit Free Press*, Detroit, Michigan. October 21, 22, 1916.

Wachter, Georgann and Mike, http://www.vaxxine.com/advtech/shipwrecks/sw2006/g&mw.htm.

## THE MYSTERIOUS SINKING OF TUGBOAT SACHEM
*Courier Express*, Buffalo, New York, December 20, 21, 23, 24, 29, 30, 1950.

*Courier Express*, Buffalo, New York, January 2, 23, 1951.

# BIBLIOGRAPHY

*Courier Express*, Buffalo, New York, March 11, 1951.

*Courier Express*, Buffalo, New York, May 27, 30, 1951.

*Courier Express*, Buffalo, New York, June 12, 26, 1951.

*Courier Express*, Buffalo, New York, August, 2, 3, 1951.

*Courier Express*, Buffalo, New York, September 23, 24, 25, 1951.

*Courier Express*, Buffalo, New York, April 7, 1952.

*Courier Express*, Buffalo, New York, December 18, 1955.

Historical Collection of the Great Lakes, Bowling Green State University.

Swayze, David D., *Shipwreck!*, Harbor House Publishers, Inc., Boyne City, Michigan, 1992.

## SABOTAGE AT THE SOO!
*Locks and Ships*, The Soo locks Boat Tours, Sault Ste. Marie.

*The Evening News*, Sault Ste. Marie, Michigan October 7, 8, 9, 10, 11, 1941.

*The Soo Locks*, http://www.geo.msu.edu/geo333/SooLock.html.

United States Army Corp of Engineers, Detroit District, Operations Technical Support. "The history of the Soo Locks", http://huron.Ire.usace.army.mil/SOO/lockhist.html.

## THE SURPRISE OF THE BIRD OF MICHIGAN CITY
Burley, Dale, *The Harbor Beach Catalog*, 1982, Harbor Beach, Michigan.

*The Huron County Tribune*, August 24, 1928.

*The Lakeshore Guardian*, July, 2001.

*The Huron County Tribune*, March 15, 1996.

## THE MANASOO CAPSIZED IN THE STORM
*The Evening News*, Sault Saint Marie, Michigan, September 18, 19, 1928.

Owen Sound Marine – Rail Museum, http://www.e-owensound.com.

## THE GOLIATH IS ON FIRE!
Mansfield, J. B., *History of the Great Lakes, Volume I*, Chicago, J. H. Beers & Company, 1899, Transcribed for the Maritime History of the Great Lakes website by Walter Lewis and Brendon Baillod, 2003.

Burkhard, Captain Ron, "*Goliath*", http://pointauxbarqueslighthouse.org.

## PARTY AT THE WILLIAM C. WARREN
Presque Isle County Advisor, Rogers City, Michigan, November 13, 20, 1947, December 3, 1947, February 30, 1948.

*The Alpena News*, Alpena Michigan, November 10, 1947.

Doner, Mary Francis, *The Salvager; The life of Captain Tom Reid on the Great Lakes*, Ross and Haines Inc., Minneapolis, Mn, 1959.

## THE STORM OF NOVEMBER 1966
Department of Transportation, Marine Board of Investigation, Marine Board of Investigation, *S.S. Daniel J. Morrell*, Sinking with loss of life, Lake Huron, 29, November 1966. Released March 4, 1968.

Hale, Dennis, Presentations by Mr. Hale. Dennis Hale, P.O. Box 104, Rock Creek, OH 44084. Authors note: If you need a Great Lakes speaker, Mr. Hale does a great job.

Hale, Dennis, Juhl, Tim, Pat and Jim Stayer. *Sole Survivor: Dennis Hale's Own Story*, Lakeshore Charters & Marine Exploration, Inc. Lexington, Michigan. 1996.

*Harbor Beach Times*, Harbor Beach, Michigan, December 8, 15, 1966, Http://web1.msue.msu.edu/iosco/nordmeer.htm.

National Transportation Board, Marine Accident Report, Released 4, March, 1968.

*The Alpena News*, Alpena, Michigan, November 21, 22, 29, 30, 1966.

*The Bay City Times*, Bay City, Michigan, November 28, December 1, 2, 3, 1966.

*The Evening News*, Sault Ste. Marie, November 29, 30, December 1, 2, 3, 5, 1966.

*The Columbus Dispatch*, Columbus, Ohio, Bernard Rogers McCoy, November 26, 2006.

*The Times Herald*, Port Huron, Michigan, Danielle Quisenberry, *"Morrell's* horror lingers four decades after sinking"* November 2006.

# ACKNOWLEDGEMENTS

No historical endeavor can be accomplished without the assistance and aid of many. I want to thank all of those who contributed.

Affholder, Roger, of the Point Aux Barques Lighthouse Society for assisting with photographs.

Bayliss Public Library and Susan James for assistance with research and access to their photographic collection.

Bowling Green State University, Historical Collections of the Great Lakes, Bowling Green State University. Robert Graham, Archivist.

Buffalo and Erie County Public Library.

Burkhard, Captain Ron, a diver, a Great Lakes writer, and a man who fights to save lighthouses.

Clark, Hugh for his assistance in Canadian geography, access to his photographic collection and for being a friend.

Conneaut Public Library, Conneaut, Ohio, Deborah Zingaro, Director, Gail Connors, Research.

DeFrain, Leonard, the Harbor Beach Historian.

Door County Maritime Museum and Lighthouse Preservation Society, Sturgeon Bay, Wisconsin, June Larson, Assistant Curator.

Gerow, Ed, for sharing his vast knowledge of the Great Lakes and ships.

Harbor Beach Public Library, Harbor Beach, Michigan. Vicki Mazure, Director.

Kimble, Jan, Historian of the Presque Isle Lighthouse.

Klebba, Ron, Harbor Beach, Michigan for his friendship and knowledge of sailing and boat construction.

Le Sault de Sainte Marie Historical Sites, Inc., Marc Svatora, Curator, Sault Ste. Marie, Michigan.

Lewis, William D., for access to his personal photograph collection.

Library of Michigan and the State of Michigan Archives, Lansing, Michigan.

Lower Lakes Marine Historical Society, Buffalo, New York.

Main, Tom and Linda, Caseville, Michigan for their assistance in sailing terminology, and technique.

Mehringer, Tom, for sharing his knowledge on the Lakes and S.C.U.B.A. diving experiences.

Milwaukee Public Library, Suzette Lopez of the Great Lake Collection.

**199**

Morden, Charlie, thanks for the use of his historical information.

Port Huron Museum. Special thanks to T. J. Gaffney, Curator of Collections, Port Huron Michigan, for his continued support.

Presque Isle Lighthouse.

St. Clair Public Library, Port Huron, Michigan.

The Grice House Museum, Harbor Beach, Michigan.

Traverse City Public Library, Traverse City, Michigan.

Toledo Lucas County Library, James Marshall, Director.

Unbehaun, Charlie, for his knowledge of diving and sharing information on wrecks.

United States Coast Guard, Historian's Office, Christopher B. Havern, Historian.

University of Wisconsin-Superior, JDH Library, Laura Jacobs.

Voelker, Chuck, for access to his personal photographic collection.

www.boatnerd.com Freighter Frank in Port Huron, Michigan.

Williamson, K. Don, for his knowledge of Great Lakes boating.

Wobser, David J., thanks for providing *Windoc* photographs.

Wicklund, Dick, Lake Lore Marine Society, for access to his personal photographic collection.

Wisconsin Maritime Historical Society, Catherine Sanders, Milwaukee, Wisconsin.

# ABOUT THE AUTHOR

Geography has played an important part in shaping Wayne "Skip" Kadar's love of the Great Lakes. Throughout his life he has lived in the downriver area of Detroit, Marquette, Harbor Beach and at the family cottage in Manistique, Michigan. Growing and living in these rich historic maritime areas has instilled in him a love of the Great Lakes and their maritime past.

This love has taken him in many directions. He is a certified S.C.U.B.A. diver and avid boater, having owned most all types of boats

*Photo by Karen Kadar*

from Personal Water Craft to sailboats to a small cruiser. He is involved in lighthouse restoration, serving as the Vice President of the Harbor Beach Lighthouse Preservation Society.

Mr. Kadar enjoys studying and researching Great Lakes maritime history and has made presentations on maritime history on a local, state and international level.

An educator for thirty years, Mr. Kadar retired after 15 years as a high school principal.

Skip lives in Harbor Beach, Michigan with his wife Karen. During the summer Skip can usually be found at the Harbor Beach Marina, on the family boat "Pirate's Lady" or at the lighthouse.

Other Wayne Kadar titles
by Avery Color Studios:

### Great Lakes Disasters

### Great Lakes Serial Killers, True Accounts of the Great Lakes Most Gruesome Murders

### Great Lakes Heroes And Villains

### Great Lakes Collisions, Wrecks & Disasters, Ships 400 To 998 Feet

Avery Color Studios, Inc. has a full line of Great Lakes oriented books, puzzles, cookbooks, shipwreck and lighthouse maps and posters.

For a free full-color catalog, call **1-800-722-9925**

Avery Color Studios, Inc. products are available at gift shops and bookstores throughout the Great Lakes region.